Gordon Wilson

An Ordinary Hero

Also by Alf McCreary

Corrymeela – The Search for Peace
Survivors
Profiles of Hope
Tried by Fire
Marie – A Story from Enniskillen (with Gordon Wilson)

Travelogues
Ulster Journey
This Northern Land

Third World
Up with People

Corporate and Institutional History
One Hundred Years of Caring
Spirit of the Age
By All Accounts
Degrees of Excellence (with Brian Walker)
On with the Show

Essays and Collected Journalism
Princes, Presidents and Punters
The Good, the Bad and the Barmy

Autobiographical
Remember When

Gordon Wilson

An Ordinary Hero

Alf McCreary

Marshall Pickering
An Imprint of HarperCollinsPublishers

Marshall Pickering is an Imprint of
HarperCollins*Religious*
Part of HarperCollins*Publishers*
77–85 Fulham Palace Road
London W6 8JB

First published in Great Britain
in 1996 by Marshall Pickering

3 5 7 9 10 8 6 4 2

A catalogue record for this book is
available from the British Library

0 551 030267

Printed and bound in Great Britain by
Caledonian International Manufacturing Ltd, Glasgow

Contents

Acknowledgements

The author and publisher would like to acknowledge the use of material from a wide range of sources, including *The Belfast Telegraph*, *Sunday Life*, *The Belfast Newsletter*, *The Irish News*, *The Impartial Reporter of Enniskillen*, *The Irish Times*, the former *Irish Press*, the *London Times*, the London *Independent*, *The Daily Mail*, and *The Sunday Times*; the proceedings of the Dail and Seanad Eireann; the BBC and Radio Telefis Eireann; Colin and Wendy Parry and the publishers Hodder and Stoughton for material from their book *Tim – An Ordinary Boy*; and the Stationery Office, Dublin and The Blackstaff Press, Belfast respectively for material from the proceedings of the Forum for Peace and Reconciliation and from 'Paths to a Political Settlement in Ireland'.

Introduction

At 2.30 p.m. on Tuesday 27 June 1995, a radio reporter rang me at my office in Belfast and said in the direct and efficient way of a journalist with a job to do, 'Gordon Wilson is dead. I would like you to pay a tribute to him.' I was still struggling to take in the news when, minutes later, the features editor from a Belfast newspaper made a similar telephone call. Then a BBC television journalist was on the line. They all wanted a tribute to Gordon Wilson, and at a moment's notice. I had been a journalist for over 30 years and knew what was required. Professionally I obliged, and felt privileged to be asked to do so. Privately, I was shocked and could barely articulate my thoughts, because I had lost a friend.

That friendship began in the late 1980s when I had been asked to write a book, with Gordon, about his daughter Marie, who had died in the IRA explosion at Enniskillen on Remembrance Day 1987. Ten other people died, and many were injured in one of the worst atrocities of the Northern Ireland troubles. Overnight, Gordon became a national and an international figure when he told a BBC reporter: *'I bear no ill-will. I bear no grudge. Dirty sort of talk is not going to bring her back to life. Don't ask me, please, for a purpose. I don't have a purpose. I don't have an answer. But I know there has to be a plan. It's part of a greater plan, and God is good. And we shall meet again.'* His words, as they were broadcast, stopped people in their tracks, and letters of sympathy and support poured in to Enniskillen and the Wilson home from around the world.

While researching and writing the book I came to know Gordon and Joan Wilson, and also their children, Peter and Julie Anne. Indeed, I was made to feel a part of the family, and when the book was published, we all hoped that it would not only pay tribute to Marie and all other victims of violence, but might also help other people who had lost loved ones.

After the initial publicity following the launch of the book, I stayed in touch with the Wilson family. I watched with admiration as Gordon, with ever-increasing effectiveness, told Marie's story to a vast audience, through television, radio, the press and particularly through an extensive and punishing schedule of speaking engagements. I also admired his courage in accepting a seat on the Irish Senate, even though he knew it would lose him some friends and would attract hostile comments. That courage and his ability to withstand severe criticism was evident in his lonely decision to seek a face-to-face meeting with the leadership of the Provisional IRA some two months after becoming a Senator.

Like all his friends, and thousands of people all over the world, I shared his immense sorrow at the tragic and untimely death of his son Peter in a car accident in December 1994. That was a blow from which Gordon never recovered, and it marked the beginning of his own end only six months later.

A short time before he died, we had made arrangements to meet later during that summer to plan his biography, which he hoped would be completed shortly after his retirement at the age of 70, some three years ahead. But this was not to be. His death cut short a remarkable mission of forgiveness and reconciliation.

In this biography I have tried to capture the many sides of Gordon Wilson, and to portray the real man behind the public image. It will be seen that he had more than a spark of the divine in him, but was also very human. He was a complex character, not just a simple do-gooder, and he would have hated any biography which presented him as other than himself, warts and all. Our friendship demanded nothing less.

In this biography I have been helped immeasurably by so many people who have taken the time and trouble to talk to me, or to write, about Gordon. Many of these people are mentioned in the text, while some wished to remain anonymous. Others meant to contribute, but were overtaken by time or the pressure of business.

Special thanks are due to a number of people: to President Mary Robinson who, despite a heavy schedule of engagements, found time to talk to me and to write the Foreword; to my wife Hilary, who sustained me through the preparation and writing of this very personal book about a special friend; to Christine Smith, my editor, whose friendship and professional help Gordon and I greatly appreciated during the preparation of the book about Marie, as I have done in writing this biography; to Pauline Allen for her invaluable help in preparing the manuscript; to Aisling Maguire, Gordon's secretary-assistant in Dublin, and Michelle Kennedy, his secretary in Enniskillen, for their insights into the public and private man; to the Reverend Jim Rea for important background information; and to Joan Wilson, her daughter Julie Anne and her daughter-in-law Ingrid, who relived painful and deeply personal memories and talked freely to me with total trust.

Joan, above all, has been a tower of strength to me, as she is to all those whose lives she touches. It is to Joan that I dedicate this biography of Gordon, with affection and respect.

Alf McCreary
Belfast, 26 September 1996

Foreword

The emergence of Gordon Wilson as hero from the rubble of Enniskillen's bombed out Cenotaph on Remembrance Sunday 1987 was as unexpected as the bomb itself. Consoling his daughter Marie as she lay gravely injured at his side and pledging forgiveness to her killers, the ordinary, hitherto unknown and instinctively private man became a public symbol of hope in an apparently hopeless time.

Democracy rests on the irreducible value of the individual person and on its sense of the difference which that individual can make. Gordon Wilson's consciousness of the value of every individual life born of the intimacy of his daughter's death awakened his sense of the difference he and other individuals could make. Without that personal acceptance of responsibility democracy cannot work. It must be complemented by the sense of solidarity which in a broken society always involves forgiveness and reconciliation. Few Irish people have grasped these basic truths about democracy as clearly, as passionately and as effectively as Gordon.

Even a person as strong as Gordon could not have achieved what he did simply on his own. His continuing inspiration was his daughter Marie whom he carried in his heart and by whose spirit he felt called to devote his life to peacemaking. His wife Joan was his true partner in this, as the rock of quiet strength who understood Gordon's need to express through word and action his commitment to securing peace and reconciliation, and who was always there to give him the comfort and support he needed. Joan and their daughter Julie Ann had to assist him later through the tragic death by accident of his son Peter. The foundation of all this was laid in the family's firm and generous Methodist faith. I was very conscious of this during the funeral services in Enniskillen for Peter and, too soon afterwards, for Gordon himself.

The peace pilgrimage on which Gordon Wilson had set out from Enniskillen took him throughout these islands and beyond. The journeying was more than geographical. The private person of unionist background was brave enough to accept a seat in Seanad Éireann in Dublin despite knowing that it would be criticized by some. His courage took him much further than that, into frustrating conversations with the paramilitaries. In the midst of his peace journeying he was called from us too soon to join Marie, Peter and his sustaining God.

In this biography, Alf McCreary reminds us of the best of our kind at a very important time. Enniskillen, which has become such a symbol of hope and reconciliation, has been attacked once more although thankfully without any death companion for Marie. As 'the darkness drops again' and 'mere anarchy' is just restrained, the memory and model of Gordon Wilson are of particular significance. The Enniskillen moment of breakthrough in such an extended period of breakdown renews our hope in civic heroes and reinforces our commitment to democratic ways. For this we should be grateful to Alf McCreary and rejoice that this account of the life and spirit of Gordon Wilson has been produced so well and so quickly.

Mary Robinson
President of Ireland
July 1996

1

Cross-Border

William Gordon Wilson was born on 25 September 1927 in Manorhamilton, a town in County Leitrim in the Irish Republic, near the border with Northern Ireland. That border had been created only a few years previously when the island of Ireland had been partitioned in the aftermath of the Irish War of Independence. The violence of Irish politics was the grim background which was to shadow the lives of the young Gordon Wilson and his contemporaries, but the early days in Leitrim were relatively trouble-free. Gordon, the eldest of four children, had a happy childhood in a strongly Methodist household, with his three sisters, Joan, Wilma and Dorothy.

Gordon's father George was born in 1897, and at the age of fifteen and a half, he began his apprenticeship as a draper. He was one of a family of six who were reared in a small three-roomed thatched cottage at Benbow Mountain, about three miles outside Manorhamilton. Money was scarce, jobs were in short supply, and several members of the family had emigrated to New Zealand or Canada, not with dreams of wealth but simply in search of a living.

George Wilson stayed in the drapery business during the First World War, and his hard work and his instinct for business paid dividends. In 1925 he bought a shop in Manorhamilton, and later on he showed his entrepreneurial flair by setting up two small local factories.

In 1926 he married Henrietta Conn from Ballykelly in County Londonderry. She had trained as a nurse in the Royal Victoria Hospital, just like her granddaughter Marie Wilson would two generations later. Henrietta, known as Etta to the family, had met George when she was a 'live-in' nurse to one of his uncles in Manorhamilton. They were married in the bride's home in Ballykelly, and after a honeymoon on Killarney – quite a 'grand' honeymoon by the standards of those times – they settled down in Manorhamilton.

Gordon had happy memories of his childhood. Money was neither scarce nor plentiful. When Gordon was born, his father took out an insurance policy for him, but one year money was so short that he had to take out a 'waiver' because he could not afford the annual premium of £28. Furthermore, he made a point of telling Gordon this. Such prudence also brought its rewards. It was a red-letter day when George bought his first car in 1938, a Ford that cost £100. But even on that memorable day, any tendency towards extravagance was firmly in check. Out for their first drive to the seaside resort of Bundoran, Gordon and his sisters were excited to find that the circus had come to town. Delighted at this stroke of good fortune, they clamoured around their father as he went to the cash desk and asked for six tickets – two adults, and four children at half price. But the ticket girl said, 'I'm sorry, there are no half-price tickets for children in the evenings. I'll have to charge you six shillings.' George Wilson's refusal was immediate and final. 'I'm not paying that!' he said, and walked away. 'We never did see the circus, and I remember thinking at the time that my father was a miserable old skinflint,' Gordon recalled. 'But that's the way it was – a couple of shillings in hard times made all the difference.' Whether by heredity or upbringing, or a mixture of both, Gordon shared his father's acumen and his success in business.

Gordon's childhood was unsullied by the bitter fruits of political and religious strife. Gordon's sister Joan (who later married Hedley Plunkett, a Methodist Minister and a Fermanagh man) recalls: 'They were great days. I remember the Annual Show in Manorhamilton, the "fair" days, and the wonderful holidays each year to places like Bundoran, Portrush and Castlerock, and also going to visit my mother's Northern relatives in Limavady, Ballykelly and Cloughmills. I also can recall cycling from Manorhamilton to visit our grandparents at the family home, Strawbrick, and bringing groceries as a present. At other times we played tennis or cycled to Fletcher's Farm to help with the haymaking. We had a great garden at Manorhamilton, and our mother grew fruit, vegetables and lovely sweet peas. Gordon, however, disliked working in the garden and was only too happy to let others do the labour!'

Gordon was educated at the Masterson Primary School, with around thirty pupils in seven classes. The teacher, Mrs Boyd, was strict, and she had an ash-plant cane, which was used often, though not indiscriminately. Gordon later remembered an incident in this strict world of learning which illustrates his early eye for detail, his feel for a situation, and his gift for story-telling. He was ten years old at the time, in his last year at the school:

Mrs Boyd lived in terror of the Inspector from the Department of Education. He was a big-shot, descending on us every year from Dublin. His brief was not only to see if the young scholars were making the grade, but also to see whether the teacher cut the mustard too. Mrs Boyd's greatest fear was that her pupils would make a fool of her in front of this important visitor. As there were only 30 of us in the entire school, we would all come under close scrutiny. So, of course, Mrs Boyd had us shaking in our shoes too, afraid of her and of the Inspector.

On that day in 1936 when the Inspector visited our little class of five, he chose Geography as the subject with which to torment us. 'In what towns in Ireland are boots and shoes made?' he barked. 'Dundalk,' answered the first lad.

Mrs Boyd smiled.

'Kilkenny,' said the second.

Mrs Boyd glowed.

'Killarney,' said I.

'No,' said the Inspector, shaking his head sadly.

Mrs Boyd's smile withered. She looked at me as if to say, 'Stupid boy! Who ever heard of shoes being made in Killarney?' I was in for a slating when the Inspector left.

Now, my father sold boots and shoes in his drapery, as Mrs Boyd knew well. When I went home for lunch that day I told my father the story of the Inspector's visit.

'Wait a minute,' my father said. Rising from the table, he went downstairs to the shop and returned carrying an invoice.

'R. Hilliard & Co. Shoes, Killarney' was written across the top of the page.

'Take that back to school and show it to the Inspector,' he said.

With great temerity I approached Mrs Boyd that afternoon and offered her my piece of paper.

'Well,' she beamed, quickly spotting an opportunity to take the credit herself. 'Wait till I show this to the Inspector!'

The Inspector looked at the invoice, and then at me, and said, 'This is the first time in 40 years of inspecting schools that I've been put right by a pupil.'

And I was in Mrs Boyd's good books for a day or two after that!

The Primary School in Manorhamilton also gave the young Gordon Wilson a background in speaking Irish, which a contemporary Protestant schoolboy in Northern Ireland would not have had. He discussed this with the presenter John Quinn in an interview on Irish radio (RTE) in 1992: 'Mrs Boyd was an Irish language fanatic, and she taught us in English and Irish. When I left primary school at the age of eleven to go to Wesley College, Dublin as a boarder, my knowledge of Irish was such that I could talk freely in that language, and I could understand the news on the radio in Irish. When I got to the college, where Irish was just another subject like French or English, they threw the grammar-book at me. That was a mistake. By the time I sat my Leaving Certificate examination, and had to pass Irish, I just scraped through. I had lost the use of Irish from the age of eleven, when I was all but thinking in Irish. I was good on grammar but the words had gone.'

Gordon's secondary schooling at Wesley College was to give him another cultural dimension which was to have significance not only then but much later in life, when he was invited by the Irish Prime Minister, Albert Reynolds, to accept a seat in the Senate (the Irish equivalent of the House of Lords). Despite having lived for nearly 40 years in the very distinct atmosphere of Enniskillen in the North, Gordon returned to Dublin with the ease of someone who had spent his formative years there at Wesley College.

'I enjoyed Wesley,' said Gordon, 'but it was hard going. The food was in short supply, for growing boys. We had bread and butter for tea most evenings, though there was a hot meal at least once a day, and twice on Sundays. About a third of the pupils were boarders, and most of these were from rural areas. For a cub like me it was a very big deal to go to Dublin city, and I warmed to it.'

When George Wilson bought a shop in Enniskillen, he asked Gordon if he would like to switch to the Royal School Portora, situated in the town, but he declined the offer. He was enjoying what he called 'the big time' too well – the excitement of the city, the company of more than 500 other pupils and the opportunity for entertainment afforded by both. He was a sound scholar rather than a brilliant one, he played a little rugby, and he made friends easily. Jack Payne, a Dublin businessman who was a contemporary and remained a lifelong friend, recalls:

At Wesley we slept on beds side by side. Gordon was popular, and his company was enjoyed by everyone. He did not stand out at school, but he was very industrious, and he was keen to get on.

However, he was anything but a 'goody-goody'. He was one of the boys, who was up to every prank, like the rest of us. But he was sensible. Even in those days he was shrewd and sharp, and he did not suffer fools gladly. Throughout our adult lives there were periods when we did not see one another for years, but we could always move back into our old relationship within minutes of meeting again. When he was thrust into the limelight after Marie's death, it was the same Gordon I had known all those years. I would not have expected anything else from him. I cannot speak highly enough of him. He always did the right thing.

Gordon's years at Wesley gave him not only a formal education, but also a new and a painful insight into some of the darker realities of Irish history. 'I learned all sorts of things,' he recalled. 'One day our history teacher, a Dr Sammy Powell, who was a Roman Catholic, told us that the next lesson was to do with Oliver Cromwell. He said: "I am not tak-ing that lesson, because I could not teach about Cromwell without showing bias. I have permission from the Headmaster to skip this, and you will have to handle it on your own."' This was something which made a deep impression on the young Gordon Wilson, and perhaps even shocked him. For the first time, the impact of history had come through to him.

The Manorhamilton of his youth had about 800 inhabitants, of whom 5% were Protestants. The Irish Republic as a whole was over-whelmingly Catholic. The local Methodist Sunday school once had up to 100 children, but these numbers dwindled to single figures by the 1940s, as the Protestant community declined. As a boy Gordon was largely unaware of the tensions which existed between the Catholic and Protestant communities, and he developed a remarkably tolerant atti-tude from his earliest years, so he may not have appreciated the sense of isolation which many Protestants in the Republic felt, because they were a minority. Indeed, it may have been that growing feeling of isola-tion, as well as sound business interests, which prompted Gordon's par-ents to move north to Enniskillen. There was also the need to provide a suitable choice of marriage partners for their children. In an age when 'mixed marriages' were frowned upon (as they still are today in many parts of Northern Ireland), it made sense to move to a community like Enniskillen, where there was more opportunity for the Wilson children to find Protestant partners.

Gordon knew that Catholic beliefs differed from those of Methodists and other Protestants, but he was taught to try to understand and respect these differences, and not to assume that either side had a God-given right to be right, and that therefore the other side must be alto-gether wrong. This conviction stayed with him throughout his life. As he saw it, the fundamental truth was that Catholic and Protestant alike were loved by the same God, who gave his Son for all, and that all could love and worship him in their different ways. As a Methodist, of course, he believed that John Wesley was right when he preached that 'All must be saved', and he felt more at home in his own tradition. Despite the different rituals used, he sometimes worshipped at Church of Ireland

and Roman Catholic services, and whatever the place of worship, he was always aware of the presence of God. However, as he grew older it began to dawn on him that deep divisions existed in Ireland. Sometimes Catholic people whom he and his family respected talked about 'non-Catholics', implying that Protestants were not part of the true Church.

At the end of the Second World War, Gordon left Wesley College. He had done reasonably well in gaining his Leaving Certificate, and his Headmaster, Dr Irwin, asked if he would consider going into medicine, if he decided against the family business. It was a flattering invitation, and he thought about it carefully.

At the end of June 1945, he was at a crossroads. There was a 'Fair Day' on 1 July, and his father was counting on him being there to help on what would be a busy trading day. Gordon said to himself, 'This is decision time. This is the day to really sort yourself out, and decide whether or not you want to make a living out of this business.' So he went to the shop, determined to test himself. By the time the shop had closed he was satisfied that this was indeed the life for him. In his youthful ignorance he felt that he had had enough formal education and was ready to make his way in the world. His parents asked him anxiously if he really wanted to try medicine, and, if so, they would do their best to support him. But his mind was made up. He'd had enough of exams and he was out to conquer the world. On 1 September 1945 he started as a trainee in the Enniskillen store, while his father ran the shop which he had retained in Manorhamilton. Gordon was full of enthusiasm, but there were a great many rough edges that needed to be knocked off.

One of those 'rough edges' was his naivety about the religious divisions in the North, where the atmosphere was very different to that in the Republic. Back in Manorhamilton he had been part of a 5% minority, but the population of the lively trading town of Enniskillen was 50% Protestant and 50% Roman Catholic.

The reality of the situation was forcibly confirmed when he found himself at the 'cutting edge' behind the counter. He learned that his father had bought the shop from a Roman Catholic. The twenty or so staff were Catholic, the customers were almost exclusively Catholic, and the purchase of the shop by a Protestant, albeit from the 'Free

State', was seen as remarkable, if not sensational in local terms. It was run by two successive Protestant managers, and later Gordon took over responsibility for the shop. He liked to think that the shop retained the loyalty of its Catholic customers and also attracted Protestant ones. But this was not easily achieved in the climate of the day.

For Gordon the fundamental word in business and in life was 'Trust'. If a man wanted to buy a shirt, and Gordon could gain a little of his trust, and sell him a shirt into the bargain – well, that was what life and business were all about. This is not to imply that Gordon considered himself any better than the next man; it was just the way he thought and worked, in a new and very different environment. He soon learned that to most of the people in Enniskillen, knowing the other person's 'Religion' was crucial and coloured their whole attitude and approach. This was true of both sides, and showed itself in so many ways. Phrases like 'He's a Protestant, you know', or 'Catholics – they're all the same' were commonplace.

The fact that the two communities in Enniskillen were almost equal in number had a moderating influence, but the truth was that there were indeed two communities, with vastly different traditions and aspirations. Relationships between Protestants and Catholics were for the most part watchfully polite and courteous, but the elements of distrust and suspicion were always just beneath the surface, and in some cases they were obvious for all to see, and were expressed unapologetically.

It soon became apparent to Gordon that this distrust and suspicion was a way of living and thinking, inherited through many generations, and the great majority wanted to stay comfortably within their own tribe, and not rock the boat. Not only did most people not know the other side's history, and what governed their thinking, but also they did not want to know. They held tight to what they sincerely believed to be right. The moderate minority who occupied the middle ground were few and far between. Some were brave enough to run for political office on this ticket, but for such people the going was hard, since they lost their credibility on both sides. Many gave up, in what seemed to them a thankless task. They just could not attract votes either in Local Government or Provincial or General Elections. But some persisted, and over the years many genuine peacemakers had an influence for good in the town and county out of all proportion to their numbers. These were the real peacemakers, people of courage, who were prepared to take the risk of being misunderstood and misrepresented.

Gordon was only eighteen when he came to Enniskillen, but he quickly learned that the best way to survive in a business which depended on trade from both sides was to keep his own counsel. He had to contain himself on occasions because he didn't see it as part of his job to stand behind a counter trying to get people's goodwill and sell them something, and then to get into an argument. He recalled, 'I realized that you weren't going to win the argument in some cases, so politics and religion weren't part of the scene. Nevertheless, I was aware very early that Protestants in Enniskillen would see me as a blow-on from the South, and therefore worth watching, maybe not to be totally trusted, even as a Protestant. "He's from the South – he wouldn't understand," they might say. And Catholics might mistrust me just because I was a Protestant, and therefore they would assume that I would take the Protestant, Unionist line. That taught me to be careful.'

Many years later he regretted this carefulness, even if it was understandable. In a paper to the Forum for Peace and Reconciliation, which was established in late 1994 following the Provisional IRA ceasefire, he was open about his own shortcomings: 'I often regret that as a young man I did not stand up and speak out against injustice and wrong when I saw them happening in my part of the world. I drew back because I regarded politicians as hard men, and I stayed comfortable. Now I hope that my words may help to soften our hearts and change the attitudes which fostered that injustice and the long years of violence in our corner of God's garden.'

Nevertheless, even then he found it very difficult when somebody would say something with which he couldn't agree. 'A decent Protestant man, for example, would say to me, "Catholics – I wouldn't trust one of them!" Even if I said nothing, my silence might be seen as agreement. But I was Gordon Wilson the businessman, and the most I would ever say in reply, if only to plant a seed of doubt, would be, "Well, I don't know that I would go all the way down the road."'

Later, in the early fifties when working in Portadown, a poor view was taken when he marched into the shop each morning with a copy of a Dublin paper, *The Irish Times*, under his arm. But there was a lighter side to such sinister realities. On one occasion two nuns came into the shop. The other assistants suggested that Gordon should serve them, as he was from the South, and they would like his Southern accent. Tall, charming and polite, he served them, and to his astonishment they placed a very big order for curtain materials for a local school. He earned a generous commission for himself into the bargain. The other assistants were quite envious – and Gordon teased them, proud of having the last word in this very local 'divide'.

The implications of such divisions would have been comical, if they had not been so sad. Shortly before he died, in his last public speech, Gordon told an audience of 1,000 people in York about the tragi-comedy that had always been part of life in Northern Ireland: 'There was this constant rubbing off or bouncing between the two communities, and I'll tell you a little story that illustrates this. We sold heavy, lambswool underwear for men. It was made in England and carried a Union Jack on the label. As a result I had decent Catholic customers who would not buy it. The English firm went out of business, and I found another company near Dublin which made a similar garment. However, each one carried a label which said 'Made in the Irish Republic', and I had decent Protestant customers who would not buy it. It sounds funny now, but it was terribly sad.'

The young Gordon Wilson was not concerned about a person's religion, but he knew that with such a view, he was in a minority. In his old-fashioned courtesy, his traditional ideas about family life and his differences with Joan when she wanted to return to work after the children were born, he was a man of his times; but he was far ahead of his times in his tolerant outlook, which he owed partly to his upbringing and partly to the educational influences which had shaped him.

He gained much insight from his parents. Joan recalls that his mother was a very upright woman. She was an absolute stickler for truth, and Gordon inherited her driving force and integrity. From his father, Gordon inherited an acutely sharp business sense, a gift for telling stories and a love of people. His father made friends everywhere – with all creeds and classes, in business, in the local church and in sport. Their home at Manorhamilton was a place where people were constantly welcomed and entertained.

Gordon also inherited an important breadth of understanding from his Southern Methodist father and his Northern Presbyterian mother. He once said: 'There was a certain balance between them, and it had to be kept all the time. That certainly had a bearing on my thinking. So, too, had Methodism. We were regular church attenders, and we were brought up very strictly, certainly by modern standards. During the war my father listened to the one o'clock news on a Sunday, but when it was over he would switch off the radio. It was the Sabbath Day, and there was no need for music.'

Gordon's strict Methodist upbringing, the differing experiences of his parents from each side of the Irish border, his schooling in Dublin, his life as part of a tiny minority in the Republic, and then having to adjust to being part of a much bigger Protestant group in the North, plus his own street-wise humour and his diplomatic skills as a businessman selling his products to both communities – all these factors combined to produce a man whose integrity remained unchanged and whose Christian hope never wavered, even when they were put to the ultimate test after the brutal murder of his daughter so many years later. The boy from Manorhamilton and the young draper from Fermanagh became the man from Enniskillen whose integrity captured the admiration of the world so dramatically from the depths of personal despair.

2

Married Life

Joan Watson and Gordon Wilson were married on 2 August 1955 in the small Methodist Church at Pubble, near Enniskillen. Gordon's friend Charlie Maguire and his cousin Francis Stewart were best man and groomsman. His sister Wilma was one of the bridesmaids, and the other was Joan's special friend from her college days, Louie Noble. The officiating Minister was Hedley Plunkett, Gordon's brother-in-law, assisted by the Reverend Harold Sloan. The small church was well-filled with a congregation singing 'Love Divine' and 'O Perfect Love' with all the verve and gusto of a Methodist congregation.

The reception for 100 people was held in the Minor Town Hall at Enniskillen. According to the custom of the times, the guest-list was drawn up by the parents. The bride and groom had little say in the matter. Gordon was almost 28, and Joan was 24. Her mother thought she was far too young to marry. Joan recalls that Gordon's speech at the reception was by far the best of the day: 'It was the first time I heard him speak in public, and I thought he was amazingly good. After all, one of the things which attracted me to him was his lovely Leitrim accent, and his courtesy. He really was a most courteous person.'

However, it was by no means love at first sight: 'The first time I saw him was outside his home at Cooper Crescent, which is still the family house. I was a school-girl at Enniskillen Collegiate, just opposite, and someone said, "There's Gordon Wilson." I spotted this fellow on a push-bike which was too small for his long legs. I was not interested in talking to boys on bikes, and, anyhow, he was not the least interested in a bunch of giggling teenagers on their way to school!'

After finishing at Enniskillen Collegiate School, Joan studied at Stranmillis Teacher Training College from 1949 to 1953. She recalls seeing Gordon at a Methodist Conference Service in Belfast with his sister Joan, but they did not meet. She also remembers seeing him at the Wilsons' shop when she went in with her mother to buy a suit for her graduation from Stranmillis.

Gordon encountered Joan again at a social evening in the local town hall, and this time he asked one of his male friends for an introduction. Though they dined at the same table, the hoped-for introduction was not made.

A few weeks later, a mutual friend (the Rev. Tom Crabbe, then a junior Methodist minister) was in a conspiratorial mood and plotted to introduce them while Gordon was playing badminton in the church hall and Joan, now an assistant teacher at Enniskillen Model School, was being shown the manuals on the organ. The organist, Richey Wilson, did not welcome any interruptions and dispatched the young minister in no uncertain terms. Undeterred, he continued to plead Gordon's cause in the Religious Instruction class which he taught at Joan's school.

But Joan ignored the hints. Her view was simple: 'If he's as keen as he makes out, let him approach me himself!' Then Gordon's sister Wilma came to his rescue. The simple fact was that Gordon was too shy to make his own advances. One day Joan was in the shop, and Wilma asked her if she would go with her to a play in the local town hall. Afterwards, Gordon met them and drove them to the Wilson family home for supper. Joan smiled at the thought of collusion, but had sufficient tact not to ask for explanations. Later he took Joan home and, plucking up courage, invited her to the cinema. Even then, their first date was at the cinema in nearby Irvinestown, for fear that they might be seen in Enniskillen. Young courting couples like to keep their secrets to themselves.

Eventually Joan told her mother about her new boyfriend. 'My mother said, "You're 22 and you should know what you are about." I brought Gordon home to meet my parents, and my father said, "That's the sort of young fellow you should be bringing home!"' In turn Joan visited the Wilson home, to mutual approval. Gordon proposed to Joan formally in November 1954, in his tiny black Morris Minor, on the picturesque shore of Lough Erne. Joan was a bit taken aback, because her career was uppermost in her mind. However, she promised to think it over quietly, and when Gordon broached the subject a few weeks later, Joan accepted. She felt a little rushed, but she also knew that Gordon was right for her.

They became engaged in January 1955, and they went by train to Belfast to buy an engagement ring. There was a great deal of frost and snow, and Gordon hated driving in such conditions. Joan remembers: 'Gordon wanted to spend over £100, which was a lot of money in those days. There was an engagement party at the Wilsons and everyone made a great fuss, except Gordon's father, who sat in a chair, reading his newspaper. When all the others had left the room he called me over to see the ring. "Long may you wear it," he remarked, and that was all he said!' He was not a man given to praise.

Joan was nervous and apprehensive about being accepted into Gordon's family, but she discovered that they were warm and welcoming. She was conscious that she came from a very different background. She was from farming stock, and she had trained as a teacher – a vocational career. She knew that she was marrying into a business family, and decided early on that she would let the Wilsons get on with it, in their own way. She was determined to maintain her own interests and career, but also to give Gordon all the moral and domestic support he needed to be successful in his business. This was not entirely Gordon's notion of marital bliss, but Joan stuck to her guns throughout their married life, holding on to her career in the face of considerable opposition from Gordon at times.

About fifteen years into their marriage, Gordon's father took Joan aside and said, 'You've made a man of my son.' Coming from someone who rarely paid compliments, that was high praise indeed. Joan grew to love her in-laws. Despite his abrupt manner, Gordon's father had a caring, loving, generous nature. His sense of humour took some getting used to, but he had a vast fund of amusing stories. Gordon inherited his father's story-telling skills and was never happier than when he had an audience around him.

Once engaged, Gordon was no longer the shy, awkward suitor. His confidence and his apparent ease in any situation continued to impress Joan. He was a natural leader, with a charisma all his own. He expected a lot from people around him, but he was always stimulating company.

Their honeymoon was spent in the Hydro Hotel in Peebles. And in time-honoured tradition, that was when they had their first row! Gordon appeared to be supremely confident when it came to finding directions, even though his family and friends knew that he was notorious for getting lost. On the way to Peebles he asked Joan to help, but then accused her of not reading the map properly. Joan says: 'He annoyed me so much that I felt like hitting him with the map. I learned throughout our married life that he always became uptight before a journey, and that a row was likely to break out about map-reading. In America he even managed to have a row with Marie, who became so fed up that she closed the map and said, "Dad, you can find your own way." I felt sorry for her, and thought of our first row about maps. It did not spoil our honeymoon, but I learned a bit more about my new husband. He simply would not be told!'

They set up home in a flat over the family shop in Enniskillen's High Street. As a couple they were well suited. Both had a strong commitment to Methodism, they were country people, and they shared an emphasis on education, on earning their own living and on being of service to people. But they were both very strong-willed characters too. She was an only child, and it was a shock after the wedding to realize that her independence had gone. No longer could she go back to her old home in Tempo and be the centre of her parents' attentions.

Gordon concentrated on building up the drapery business, and Joan carried on her music-teaching career in Enniskillen Model School until Peter, their first child, arrived on 11 July 1956. Joan had intended to return to teaching after Peter's birth, but Gordon had other ideas. He was of the old school who believed that a woman's place was to be at home with her children. Joan was adamant, however, and would have had her way but for the fact that when Peter was born, she could not bear to leave him. Surprised at the strength of feeling which overwhelmed her, she resigned from her job. She missed her teaching, but she did not need Gordon to tell her that she was doing the right thing by staying at home with their son.

Gordon was a shrewd businessman with a great deal of entrepreneurial flair. They did not need to worry about losing an extra salary, although Joan had always enjoyed her independence. He held sales several times a year and prepared for them meticulously. Each year the takings went up, and that gave him great satisfaction. But he was not a man driven by money. He liked to 'make ends meet', but he used to say that health and happiness were much more important.

He had an eye for a good deal, and, as in many other aspects of his life, he was decisive. Joan recalls, 'He had a precision about him. Gordon did not like people dithering about. His policy was "Make up your mind and stick to it" – and there was no going back on your word. In business he did not haggle. If things were at the price he had set, that was the price you paid.'

However, there were exceptions. Henry Keys, now Methodist Chaplain at the Queen's University in Belfast, remembers going as a boy into Wilson's shop in Enniskillen: 'It was a place where you were always made to feel welcome. I can still see the three of them in my mind's eye – the old man Wilson, Gordon and his son Peter. And they all had the knack of selling you something. I remember Gordon's big, long, loping stride. He seemed to move down the whole length of the shop in a couple of seconds. He knew my family and he was aware that I was a young student training for the Methodist ministry. So he often knocked a few bob off whatever I was buying. I don't know whether it was that, or the friendliness of the Wilsons, but I always left their shop feeling that my visit had been really worthwhile.'

Father Brian D'Arcy, a former Superior of the Passionist Monastery in Enniskillen, and a well known freelance journalist and broadcaster, also remembers Gordon the businessman, who managed to please customers on all sides and who showed no partiality: 'My first memory of Enniskillen was coming in as a young fellow from the country and walking up and down the streets of the town, on my way to St Michael's College. To me, that was like going to the ends of the earth at that time. Wilson's was a place where both Protestants and Roman Catholics would shop, and that was unusual enough for Enniskillen in the mid-fifties. Gordon Wilson quite often would be standing in the door of his shop, and he would always say, 'Hello sonny' to you. 'Sonny' was not a word that was used in Enniskillen, so he would have brought it with him, from his Manorhamilton background.

'He was a friendly, big man. When you are growing up, a big man looks twice as big! I noticed that he had rather large hands. I got to the stage where I used to reply, "Hello, Mr Wilson." He never knew who or what I was; to him I was just "sonny", and he would talk to me – which not all Protestant shopkeepers in the town would do to a young lad wearing the uniform of a local Catholic school. Eventually I left Enniskillen, and I didn't have much contact with him, although members of my family would always tell me about shopping at Wilson's. The next time I was in contact was after Marie died, when I expressed my sympathy to him. Again I met that man who had the seeds of being friendly and open, and speaking and talking to you – that seed having fructified into something special.'

Gordon was a very good boss and saw the staff point of view, and was highly regarded by both customers and staff. He was able to sort out any disagreement between customer or assistant. It didn't matter who the customer was: he was the same to everybody, and he liked his staff to treat all customers equally and with respect.

The day after he died, a lady came to Joan's door. She said, 'I used to work in the shop, and I would like to go to the church and put some flowers in the porch in memory of a good boss. He was one of the most honourable men I have ever met – you could not tell him a lie.' From the message boy up, his staff knew that he was straight and fair. He took no nonsense. Unfortunately, there were times when he had to sack people, but he did this as carefully and sympathetically as he could.

Gordon's sister Wilma worked with him for some 30 years: 'During those years we had a great relationship. He was always willing to listen to your point of view, and to give his opinion. Gordon was at his desk early and liked his staff to be at the counter in good time. He was a great time-keeper and did not like to be kept waiting. When he said 9.00 a.m. he meant it!

'Sale times in the shop! We had four sales during the year – that was what Gordon liked best. He would spend a long time getting all the senior members of staff ready for the opening day. Windows, paper advertisements and all sale items had to be ready for the 9.15 a.m. deadline. He would go down to open the doors with his usual long strides and he would say, "All ready for the rush, Wilma!" And, mind you, we had to be ready! And with each department trying to outdo the other, he got the best out of us all.'

One day he had spent twenty minutes with a customer while she was choosing a cotton reel costing just a few pence to match a curtain she was making (she hadn't even bought the material in the shop). At the finish he went to Wilma and said, 'There must be an easier way to make a bob or two than selling a reel of thread!' That was when he would get a little frustrated and would say, 'You can't win 'em all!'

Business life was not always easy. Gordon had his worries, like everyone else. At one stage he planned a major renovation of the shop – an enormous undertaking. Until it was completed, he took the worry of it home with him. And although it worked out successfully and he was not a worrier by nature, and believed in crossing bridges when he came to them, he still drove himself hard. By the age of 36 he had an ulcer. He went into hospital, where he was told take things easier.

Gordon's strongly competitive nature and his driving, restless energy found another outlet – in sport. Like his father, who had been a champion fisherman and had represented Ireland, he did not do things by halves. However, fishing held no charm for Gordon, and on one early outing with his father, he studiously ignored the rod and line and buried himself in a book. Later he turned to badminton, bowls, rugby and golf. He played bowls for Ireland several times, but once he began to lose the fine edge of a potential champion he gave it up completely. He recalled: 'One evening I was due to play against a lady who was a useful bowler, but I thought that I would win without much trouble. As it happened I couldn't do a thing right, and on the night she beat me. So I packed it in, there and then. There was no point in messing about, and anyway I had been devoting an awful lot of time to the bowls which I should have been spending with my family.' Part of the truth was that Gordon was not a good loser. He hated doing things badly, he liked to win, and he could not stand being beaten by a woman!

He played a great deal of golf in later years, and he had a regular game with Enniskillen friends every weekend at Murvagh in Donegal. He was a keen golfer, but his skills were somewhat limited. He would have been more than pleased to know that he would be remembered publicly as 'one of the best golfers in the country' in a posthumous tribute by one church leader. His golf was a bitter-sweet experience, as it is to many players, but it also became a kind of therapy – first away from the strains of business, and then after the trauma of Marie's death.

Joan was not impressed by Gordon's aggressive determination, nor by the agonizing post-mortems whenever he had lost. 'At first he played badminton a lot, but as I was busy preparing my lessons for school, I did not often see him play. When I did, I was shocked! He was so aggressive! I asked myself, "Was this the man I married?" It was the same on the golf course. He had to win, although he was not a good golfer. When he had not been playing well, he would come home depressed. You would think he had been playing in the Ryder Cup! I used to get fed up with these post-mortems, and it became worse as he got older, because his golf got worse! If he did not play well, it was an absolute disaster for him. Despite all this, I encouraged him because it got him out in the fresh air and away from the pressures of the business. And I encouraged him to go abroad for a week's golfing each year with his friends. That did him good, and he came back refreshed.'

After Marie's death, the popular media portrayed Gordon as a saint. He could charm anybody, and when they were in Dublin at Senate functions and other gatherings, the women would say to Joan, 'Mrs Wilson, your husband is a *beautiful* man!' She would reply, 'I'll be the judge of that – I live with him!' Of course, he was a 'beautiful man' in many ways, but Joan knew that he was no saint. He could lose his temper, he could be impatient, and he was always in a rush. Gordon was always chasing her on when she wanted to stay back and dream. On one holiday when they visited a French chateau, he laid down a time to leave the place, and when the time came she felt that she had hardly seen a thing. And yet if it came to watching golf he could wait around all day. That used to make Joan very agitated, and she would think that their marriage was not balanced.

Although he was kind, caring and supportive as a husband, he also liked to get his own way. 'Anything for a quiet life' was not his motto. As an only child, Joan had got her own way at home often enough, but not in her marriage. She had to learn to stand her ground.

Gordon hated household chores. He disliked gardening, except cutting the lawn, in which he took an inordinate, if somewhat unjustified, pride. He would say, 'Joan, that lawn looks well after it is cut,' and Joan would retort, 'And who did the edges and the shrubs?' Gordon had always been used to having things done for him, even at home, where there was always a daily help. He was hopeless about the house. If Joan was away from home she would leave him something to eat, but he would almost always go to the neighbours and invite himself for a meal. He could make tea and warm up soup – that was about it. Julie Anne used to scold her mother about it. She would say, 'You're far too soft with him. You haven't trained him properly!'

The truth was, Gordon intensely disliked being alone, but thrived in company. He had no interest in learning self-sufficiency. He could become depressed on his own, and needed people around him. He was a natural raconteur, and he liked an audience, especially for his humour. He was a big-hearted, out-going man who liked people, and they liked him. At a party, he used to come into his own. Joan, lacking his confidence and ease, would say to him, 'Don't leave me here on my own', and he would promise to stay beside her. Inevitably he would be drawn away, and she would have to make her own conversations with people around her. When he returned he would say, 'Sure, I knew you could manage very well!'

Their marriage was strong, but their differences surfaced every now and then. Whenever they had rows, Gordon would leave Joan to cool down, whereas she expected him to make overtures of peace. And eventually he would frustrate her further by saying, 'What has offended you?' as if nothing in the world was wrong. Neither Joan nor Gordon gave in easily. Gordon's manifest impatience irked Joan greatly from time to time, but she often chose to let him have his way. However, there were fundamental points and issues where she drew the line, such as maintaining her own career, interests and sphere of influence, and in later years she insisted that he took better care of his health. In the early days, Joan's teaching was a bone of contention, since Gordon thought that a woman's place was in the home. But Joan gradually cured him of that, and as their own children grew older, he began to appreciate the importance of education.

But Gordon was indeed the right man for Joan, as she recollects: 'Gordon taught me many things. I was a dreamer, but he wakened me out of my dreams. I learned to be on time, to say what I really meant, and not to be afraid of people. I had been a bit sheltered, and he gradually drew me out. We met so many people, and that gave me confidence. Above all, he taught me the power of love. Right from the early days, Gordon always spoke about love. He always said, "The bottom line is love." He practised it all his life. He understood it when we were married; it seemed to be a part of his everyday life. Many a time I would go into a tizz about something, and he would say, 'We have to show true love.' He didn't preach, but he showed love in the simple things.

'I knew before we were married that he was a churchgoer, but I cannot recall his Christianity growing out of a Damascus-road experience. It was a gradual deepening. He loved the Wesley hymns. I was not much impressed, but he shared their beauty with me, and I have liked them ever since. Gordon taught me that love mattered, that you aired your views and you weathered storms together. We learned to share our troubles, and there were no secrets. There was love and trust, and as the years went on we got to know one another better and better. We were fortunate in that we were friends.'

Although he liked getting his own way and could be stubborn, Gordon was always aware of the enormous strength and support of Joan, who in many ways was the 'engine' of the family. Gordon, despite his old-fashioned attitudes to marriage and his inherent chauvinism, was exceptionally attentive, kind and supportive in his own way. Joan and Gordon's marriage was a good example of two very strong-minded people learning to live together and creating a very special bond, and with it a happy home.

Joan felt that her mission was to keep the home going and to provide Gordon with rest and relaxation, in order to give him strength for his work and his calling. 'I remember as a young girl praying to God, in a way that might now seem silly, for the "right" young man to share my life. And the Lord did not let me down. Gordon and I went through so much together, and I don't know how we would have managed without each other. He was a wonderful husband and friend.'

3

Family Values

Gordon, Joan and Peter, who was now a toddler, moved from the flat over the drapery shop to what is still the Wilson family home, a large and light-filled house on a hill, not far from the centre of Enniskillen. Gordon was finding his feet in the business and Joan had resumed her career as a teacher. To the outside world they were a typically hard-working young couple, very much in love and with hardly a care. But they had already tasted the kind of tragedy that was to overshadow their lives. In June 1958, Richard, their second son, was born. He lived only two and a half hours.

Richard was born prematurely. Joan was so ill that she was not allowed to see him, and Gordon had to deal with everything. At two o'clock in the morning, summoned by a telephone call from Gordon, their minister arrived to baptize the little baby before he died. The grandparents were distraught. Joan remained in bed at the flat, where Richard had been born, and although Gordon was in deep shock, the arrangements for the funeral fell to him. He chose a small white coffin, and the grandfathers decreed that the baby should be buried in Joan's family graveyard at Tempo. Dazed the whole time and unable to be at her son's funeral, Joan recalls few details but remembers Gordon crying.

The trauma inflicted deep wounds. 'All that summer I could not bear to go near the graveyard, but after a few months Gordon took me there. We were out driving in the area, and he said, "Joan, I think you're ready to see where we laid the baby." So I went with him and looked at the little boy's grave. It was terrible. Even though this happened a long time ago, I still think about it and a feeling of great sadness comes over me at what might have been. I don't think that people ever get over the premature death of a baby. Gordon often talked about it, and all our children were told in due course about the death of baby Richard.' Joan still visits Richard's grave.

Peter was 23 months old by this time, and it was caring for him and watching his play and development that helped Joan to overcome her profound sense of loss. She realized that she had to pick herself up and give some support to Gordon, who was grieving as deeply as she was. It was this tragic experience which brought out a side of Gordon which she had not previously known. She felt his deep care for her, as well as his love. Despite his own grief, which he only expressed behind closed doors, he was a pillar of strength for Joan to lean on. She talked to her mother-in-law about her surprise at Gordon's depth of emotion. Granny Wilson told her that on the night Peter was born in a local nursing-home, having been phoned at 4.00 a.m. and told that he had a son, Gordon had gone to his room, where she could hear him crying with relief. He freely admitted to Joan later that he had 'cried like a child with relief and joy'.

When Marie died, the world thought that this was their first family tragedy, and when Peter was killed in a car crash, many people commiserated on the death of their only son. 'They were wrong,' says Joan. 'Our first tragedy was the death of Richard. I am convinced that it was the power of God which helped to pull me through, as it has done ever since, and certainly after the deaths of Marie, Peter and Gordon. When Richard died prematurely, I felt that God helped to slow me down, to take more rest, to take more care of myself, and to realize that life is so precious. When you are young you tend to take these things for granted.'

Less than two years later, joy came again into the Wilson household when Julie Anne was born on 25 May 1960. Marie followed seven years later, on 29 April 1967. Each grew up to be a very different character. Peter was a nervous child with a streak of stubbornness, but with a measure of his father's charm and good humour. His parents and teachers knew that he could be coaxed but not driven into doing something he did not like initially. Like any schoolboy, he enjoyed a prank, such as trying to make his best friend's mother lose her composure when the Moderator of the General Assembly came to tea (she was the wife of the local Presbyterian minister). Peter was also reckless on his bike and was the terror of old ladies who, when out for a walk, used to fear this long-legged youngster who would speed past them much too close for comfort. Unlike his father, Peter loved fishing, and spent hours with his grandfather and the local fishermen and the old characters from around Manorhamilton.

Peter inherited his father's craggy looks, his square-set jaw and broad face, his long, loping stride, and his firm handshake. But he was very much his own man. As the third generation of Wilsons, he showed flair and dedication in the family business, in which he played a crucial part. To some extent, however, he lacked his father's outgoing, talkative nature and his hard business edge. Peter was more of a background man, gentler and more artistic. He inherited these qualities from his mother. But he was by no means a soft touch. He had his own quiet firmness and, like many a son, he did not always see eye to eye with his father. At times he felt that Gordon was not giving him sufficient freedom in the business, but he remained loyal. There were times, however, when his father's word was law. Sometimes the others would challenge Gordon or try to get around him, but Peter never took that line. He used to say, after a difference of opinion with his father, 'That's it – the book is closed!'

Julie Anne, the middle child, was very like her father. She inherited his directness and economy of expression. Even as a child she knew her own mind, and she was very much her own person. Like Gordon, Julie Anne did not suffer fools, and she was not prone to flattery. She said what she meant, and she meant what she said. Like Gordon, she was fair and generous with praise when praise was due. On occasions it was Julie Anne who took on Gordon, and she was willing to confront him if she felt it was necessary. In later years, it was she who warned him that he was doing too much.

Nevertheless, Julie Anne was close to her father, particularly as a child. 'I was close to my mother in the way that daughters are, but Dad was the one you went to if you wanted "real" advice. I suppose we held him in awe. Certainly, we thought the world of him. Marie told him everything, and maybe she was closer to him than I was. She would talk, whereas I was not like that – I was a bit of a closed book. I did feel a bit left out, but that was my own fault, part of my own persona. I could tell a total stranger anything, but not my family. That was just me!'

Because of the demands of the business and his numerous other interests, Gordon was often an absent father. After the family meal, he was almost always dashing somewhere else – to bowls, to church, or to some other institution or organization in which he was involved. It was Joan who seemed to be there for the children, although Gordon, at the head of the table, regaling his family with the 'crack' of the day, made mealtimes one of Julie Anne's most vivid childhood memories.

What he lacked in time for his children, he more than made up for in treats for the family. Holidays were a real highlight, and the children visited America, Scandinavia, Russia and France – exotic and expensive destinations in those days. But Gordon enjoyed being the generous father, creating memories that even the tragedies which lay in the future could not take away. They felt that they were an ordinary, happy family, and such simple but solid qualities would stand them all in good stead in the years to come.

Gordon was not so engrossed in his work that there was no time for his children in it. Julie Anne remembers his delight whenever they called in on him at his office. Such was the unconditional welcome that the shop seemed like a second home to them. And they were an audience for his humour and the stories that inevitably flowed. 'I was walking down the shop and saw this customer who seemed to be looking for help. So I said, "What can I do for you?" She replied, "I'm only looking." And I said, "Well, Missus, there's no charge for looking, but there's no profit either!"' Like his father before him, Gordon loved the 'crack', the repartee.

Julie Anne recalls, 'My father was deeply Christian, and I liked his brand of religion. He did not preach, he was not a "pain in the neck" about his beliefs. Church meant a lot to him, but there was an earthiness about him which I liked. He could use strong language when he wanted to. In that sense he was a real, human, down-to-earth Christian. I admired him very much.'

Her parents were strict, she remembers: 'You did not say to Dad, "I'm going to the disco" – you asked him, "Can I go?" Marie was more inclined to be up-front about this than I was. What irritated me was the fact that I wasn't allowed to go, even though I didn't really want to go in the first place! However, the strict upbringing didn't do us any harm.'

Julie Anne went to teacher-training college at Stranmillis in Belfast. She remembers: 'Dad said, "The next three years will be the best of your life." In fact, it wasn't quite like that. I didn't know myself – I was neither a "wild woman" nor a girl from the "Bible belt". I enjoyed my course, and ended up as a teacher, living at home. Dad was proud of me, and I think he would have liked to have heard more about what I was doing, but I didn't tell him a lot. The year before the bomb, I got my own house, and that was the best thing I ever did. I had more space to myself, and I became more of my own person.'

One of the good things about living near home was the fact that Julie Anne could see Marie when she came home at weekends from her nursing in Belfast. 'I was seven years older, but we were close, even though the gap can be quite large at that age. It all seems so long ago. Now I am so sad that she is not around as my sister and friend, and that she is not able to enjoy my children. It all seems so unfair.'

Marie, as the youngest child, had a special place in the family, and her brother and sister doted on the 'baby' of the house. Even as children they used to take her out in her pram. She was a smiling and friendly child, and from an early age she displayed a strong talent for music. Joan remembers her playing 'Twinkle, twinkle, little star' on a small violin and performing in the local Methodist Church at an early age. She was not academically outstanding, but she was bright enough to pass the eleven-plus examination and take her place at Enniskillen Collegiate Grammar School, across the street from the Wilsons' house. At the Collegiate, Marie took part in school sports, sang in the school choir and became a prefect, and eventually Deputy Head Girl. She continued taking violin lessons with her mother and eventually played in the Western Area Youth Orchestra, and later with the Studio Symphony Orchestra in Belfast. She was particularly fond of singing, and at school she played the part of the Fiddler in *Fiddler On The Roof*. When she was a nurse in Belfast, she also sang in the Royal Victoria Hospital Choir.

Her decision to become a nurse may have been partly due to the earlier influence of her paternal grandmother, herself a nurse, and partly due to her desire to help people. Her Christianity developed from an early age, and a number of private notes which her parents discovered after her death indicated that she had a deep commitment to the Christian way of life. She was affected profoundly by documentaries on the Holocaust and other atrocities, but she rarely talked about the Troubles, which brought such horror and bitterness to her native land. Her father once recalled: 'She asked me, "Daddy, what's wrong with Roman Catholics?" I replied, "There's absolutely nothing wrong with Roman Catholics. Why on earth are you asking me that?"' It was something she had picked up from outside. Over the years Marie was aware that some people thought less well of Roman Catholics, but she never let anything like that interfere with her work or her life. Like father, like daughter.

But Marie was no plaster saint; there was a rebellious, tomboy side to her nature. Often she would vent her feelings about sudden challenges or setbacks, such as having to wear a 'horrible' costume in a school musical, or not being allowed to go to a disco. Such upheavals or disappointments would lead to tears and, on occasions, to running upstairs and slamming her bedroom door. But if she felt that she had been wrong, she would soon apologize. She was, in fact, a very normal teenager, and it was a wise parent who once remarked that most of the problems of a fifteen-year-old are solved by becoming a sixteen-year-old!

Gordon talked fondly about one or two of his 'battles' with the teenage Marie: 'I remember that one evening at the tea-table she asked if she could go to a disco in the local church hall. She must have been only fifteen or sixteen at the time, and I thought she was too young to go. So my answer, sadly, had to be "No". Well, the floods of tears poured forth, and off she went to her bedroom. I thought it over and felt that maybe there should be some compromise. I went up to her room and put forward the proposal that she would be allowed to go, provided that I would go with her. Naively, I thought that I could chat to the local minister at one end of the hall while Marie enjoyed herself with all the other young folk at the other end. She took one look at me and said, "Dad, you must be mad!" And that was the end of the matter.'

Gordon told another story which showed a different side to Marie, and which impressed him deeply. He talked about it to the interviewer John Quinn on the RTE programme *My Education* shortly before he died: 'She said to me, "One of my friends is celebrating her sixteenth birthday today and we're having tea down-town." So I gave her a fiver. "Big deal!" she said. "That's not enough – we might be going to the pictures." So generous Joe here put his hand in his wallet and gave her another fiver. I asked, "What's on at the cinema?" She replied, "It's only the pictures." I said, "If it's anything messy, or not right, I hope you'll use your own judgement about going." So off she went. About five minutes to eight the doorbell rang. It was Marie. She said, "Dad, I didn't like the look of it," and she put a fiver back in my hand. I asked her, "What about your friends? Did they go?" She said, "Oh, yes." I told her to keep the fiver. It struck me that it must have taken an awful lot of courage to turn on her heel and not go into that cinema, even though her friends were going ahead with it. It would have taken some guts from a fifteen-year-old to say to two sixteen-year-olds, "I'm not going, even if you are." But that was Marie.'

The special relationship between father and daughter lies at the heart of the Gordon and Marie Wilson story. Though Gordon loved all his children deeply, there was a particular intimacy with Marie, perhaps because she was so open with him, and partly because she was the 'baby' of the family. And when she lay dying under the rubble of the explosion at Enniskillen, her last words burned an indelible impression on his heart, mind and soul. 'Daddy, I love you very much' were the last words he heard her say, and he carried them with him at all times afterwards – during his many radio and television interviews, during his numerous talks to groups both large and small in every corner of the British Isles and beyond, during his face-to-face meeting with the Provisional IRA, during his speeches in the Irish Senate and at the Forum For Peace and Reconciliation, during his meetings with the Queen, with President Mary Robinson, with political leaders in London, Dublin and elsewhere, and in private conversation with colleagues and friends. Those words, and all they meant, were the cornerstone of his philosophy and of his very life. They went with him to his grave, and yet they live on.

During the preparation of the book about Marie after her death, he talked a great deal about the bond that existed between them. This was how he described it:'As her father, I felt a special bond, possibly because she was the youngest. It was the kind of relationship which you couldn't measure, and certainly she was not any closer to me than any other member of the family. I remember Marie, even as a toddler, meeting me in the hall of our house when I came in from work in the evening. She would say, "Hello, Dad," and I would more often than not take her up in my arms. She was a good girl, and lots of fun, with a great deal of love in her. The close affinity between us continued, right to the day she died. Every weekend when she was at home she would come into our bedroom and lie on the covers and chat to me about the events of the week. We were able to talk like that, on a similar wavelength, and, looking back, it was a most important part of our lives, even though, perhaps like many another father and daughter, we did not think especially of it at the time. We got on well together, and that was more than enough.'

Joan has her own perspective on the relationships in the family: 'Gordon was a very good father, but he was almost too good. He spoiled them all. He took no nonsense, but he used to let them off the hook in ways of which I would not have approved. For example, he would have let them go off to meet their friends, without practising their music or finishing their homework. That used to annoy me, perhaps because it was a bit of the schoolteacher coming out in me. But Gordon, though strict in so many ways, let them off with a lot!

'He gave us all wonderful holidays. We went to exotic places abroad, but we also took some holidays nearer home. I recall Julie Anne harping on at him about buying a caravan, and eventually he gave in, even though he didn't like caravanning. One year we went to Portrush, and on the journey there it poured with rain. He tried to drive into the caravan park but took the wrong entrance, and damaged the skylight of the caravan. The rain kept coming in, and we had to get tarpaulins to fix the leak. It was an awful nuisance. Added to that, Gordon kept banging his head on the caravan door, being so tall, and he grumbled and grumbled about it the whole time. What amazes me now is the fact that he kept it for four years, before he sold it.'

He had his regrets as a father. Joan says: 'One of the things he deeply regretted was not going to Julie Anne's graduation at Queen's University, Belfast, when she was awarded a Bachelor of Education. It was on the same day as the opening of a summer sale in the shop, and the sale was a big event for Gordon. He was in his element. It was only afterwards that he regretted not being at Queen's for Julie Anne. I think he felt it particularly when he went to Marie's nursing graduation ceremony. Julie Anne, however, understood his dilemma.'

Sometimes Gordon could be very angry. During a family holiday in France, Peter – then only nineteen – was parking Gordon's new Jaguar at St Malo. Peter forgot to put on the hand-brake, and the car slid forward and hit a wall. There wasn't much damage done, but the impact knocked off the bright silver Jaguar on the bonnet. Gordon was absolutely furious, and gave Peter a dressing-down in English, in the midst of all the French holiday-makers! Marie was in floods of tears, and poor Peter was absolutely shattered. He wasn't allowed to drive the Jaguar for the rest of the holiday. Gordon refused to talk about it for the remainder of the evening, but he was back to normal the next day!

Alan Hanna, the Methodist minister in Enniskillen from 1966 to 1974, knew the Wilson family well. He recalls Joan and Gordon as members of the church who were 'most loyal, sound, sensible, practical and very kind. Joan's musical gifts, and all her talents, were for the service of the church, and Gordon was on the main committees. He spoke his mind in a helpful way, but did not push himself forward.' Gordon served in a number of posts, including Secretary of the Board. 'Gordon and Joan were generous in heart and practice. When we arrived in Enniskillen we booked Joan to teach our daughter the piano. When I wanted to pay, at the end of the first term, all such thoughts were brushed aside by Joan. She said, "We have a minister and his wife whom we appreciate, so why should we not do something for them?" I like to think that their appreciation was partly linked to the fact that I did not remain silent about the ways in which our Protestant folk were being unjust to others.' Sometimes Gordon chatted to his minister about business affairs. He had two different attitudes. He felt strongly that his father had built up the business, starting with little or nothing. He felt that if he was worth his salt, he should leave something more behind. But a number of times he expressed the wish that he would love to hand over the whole lot, and have a small curtain-materials shop run by himself and just one assistant.

But clouds were gathering around the Wilsons and every family in Northern Ireland. The Troubles were erupting, and one day there was a Protestant-Loyalist march through Enniskillen. One of the men near the front was a local Methodist carrying his Bible. There were young men in pseudo-military dress and wearing balaclavas. It was an ominous sight. Gordon confided to his minister that he had watched the march go past his shop, then went straight to the toilet and was literally sick. Perhaps he had some idea of what that march was portending. He undoubtedly felt a revulsion towards all that it stood for.

Those were indeed ominous times. When the latest round of the Northern Ireland Troubles erupted in the late sixties, few people expected that they would continue for more than 25 years. Successive British governments tried in vain to produce a political settlement which would have the approval of both the Protestant and the Roman Catholic communities. Meanwhile, the violence escalated, with atrocity after atrocity. With no prospect of any end in sight, many people left Northern Ireland, and others contemplated doing so – not only to escape from the violence and the daily news-diet of suffering and carnage, but also to make a fresh start for themselves and their families.

Gordon was one of those who considered moving away. He recalled: 'The future really looked bleak and I began to say to myself, "Maybe it's time to pull up the stumps and go." This was something I had thought about, from time to time. And I'm sure that many other families did the same. So we began to talk about *where* we might go rather than *if* we might go.' He seriously considered selling his Enniskillen shop and taking the family to live in Scotland. It seemed to make sense, but on the way back from a visit to Scotland, he began to think about the difficulty of tearing up the family roots. 'The nearer I got to Enniskillen, the more I felt I was coming back among friends – to church and home, the Golf Club, the Rotary Club, and all the familiar touchstones of life. And I realized that nowhere else in the world would match up to the setting of Enniskillen, with its lakes, its hillsides and its gorgeous scenery. So even before I turned my car into the driveway of my home, I had come to realize that Scotland was not the place for us. We talked it over, and as a family we decided to stay.'

The die was cast, and the Wilsons stayed put in Fermanagh. The family was happy, the business was prospering, Gordon was a stalwart of the local community – President of the Rotary Club, the Golf and Bowling Clubs and the Chamber of Commerce, and also a pillar of the local Methodist Church. Like many another Ulster family, the Wilsons' roots went deep, and although the Troubles were distressing, depressing and demoralizing, they were not touched directly. For people outside Northern Ireland it was difficult to understand why all sensible people did not want to get out of the Province permanently, but for those who lived there, life appeared comparatively normal, provided they were not living in the middle of a continually troubled area. And Ulster people on both sides were not the kind of folk to be intimidated by violence into leaving the land of their birth. Gordon and Joan and their children were typical of most Northern Ireland people, who occasionally feared the worst, but generally hoped for the best. There was little that they could do to stop the violence, or to help provide a political breakthrough. What they could do was to live as normal a life as possible, and to help build up better community relations by being at peace with all their Protestant and Roman Catholic neighbours.

In family terms, there was only one small cloud on the horizon. In 1986 Gordon suffered a minor stroke, but this was treated successfully. On 25 September 1987 he reached a personal milestone when he celebrated his sixtieth birthday. The family held a party, and the children bought a golf trolley for this 'grand old man of the course'. Marie came home from the Royal Victoria Hospital, Julie Anne was there, and so was Peter and his wife Ingrid. It was a happy and relaxed occasion, just like any special birthday party. They were not to know that it was also the last gathering of the entire Wilson family. Within two months, a Provisional IRA bomb at the Enniskillen Cenotaph would tear the family apart, and life would never be the same again.

4

Carnage at the Cenotaph

8 November 1987, the day of the Enniskillen bomb, was cold and blustery. Remembrance Day is always a sombre occasion, as people honour
the dead and injured from two World Wars, and from many other con-
flicts around the globe. In Northern Ireland there was added poignancy
as the bitter and violent local conflict in which thousands of men,
women and children had been murdered and maimed since the outbreak
of the latest Troubles in 1968 was recalled. There had been explosions
in public buildings, bars and restaurants; there had been no-warning
car-bombs in busy streets; civilians had been shot dead in their own
homes in front of their families; workmen had been ordered out of their
van on a lonely country road and mowed down mercilessly by unknown
assailants; and the bloody and unwinnable war of attrition between terrorists on both sides and the security forces continued unabated. Even
more depressing was the unlikelihood of any cessation or diminution of
the violence. Remembrance Day in 1987 was yet another reminder to
the people of Northern Ireland that they had experienced so much
bloodshed, suffering and misery that it seemed things could not get
worse. By the end of that awful day, the entire community was plunged
into further shock and grief by the Provisional IRA bomb explosion
which plumbed new depths of bloodshed and depravity.

On that morning, the Wilsons busied themselves like any normal
family. Joan was making the breakfast and finalizing in her mind the
details of the music she was due to play at the organ of the local
Methodist church. Gordon was taking out his heavy dark overcoat to
protect himself against the expected chill at the Cenotaph Service. He
used to call it his 'funeral coat' – such a garment was part of the

wardrobe of almost every countryman in Ulster, where paying respects at the funeral of a friend, or even a friend of a friend, or an acquaintance, remained a widespread social custom. It was part of the extended-family dimension of local life, and also evidence of the caring and friendly nature of Ulster people. Outsiders to Northern Ireland – and many insiders as well – find it difficult to understand how such sympathy and such savagery can exist side-by-side.

Marie had come home for the weekend from the Royal Victoria Hospital in Belfast. She was getting ready to go with her father to the Cenotaph, and she took care to dress appropriately for such a solemn occasion, but underneath the dark rain-coat she wore a pink dress. Here was a girl who was full of vitality, getting on with her life, despite the backdrop of violence and death. Julie Anne was by this time living in her own house elsewhere in Enniskillen. Several miles away, in Pubble, Peter's wife Ingrid was preparing a lunch for her parents and in-laws, as well as her own family, and was putting two ducks into the oven before leaving for church with Peter and their young daughters, Judith and Eloise.

Gordon was always fussy about time-keeping, and as he and Marie left for the Cenotaph to be in good time for the ceremony, Joan looked out of the window at the blustery weather and called to Marie, 'Have you an umbrella?' She replied, 'Of course I have. Don't fuss!' Those were the last words her mother would hear her say. Gordon and Marie drove to the centre of Enniskillen and parked near the Cenotaph. It was part of an annual ritual for Gordon, and it had deep personal significance for him. Joan's father had served in the First World War and had lost a leg as a result of active service in France. Gordon once said: 'I used to make a point of going to the Cenotaph, partly because of Joan's father and also to thank, at least once a year, all the others – including my friends – who went out to risk life and limb. Some of them never came back.' Those who risked life and limb did so voluntarily. There was no compulsion, since conscription did not apply in Northern Ireland.

There was yet another dimension to Remembrance Day in Northern Ireland. Traditionally, it was regarded by many Irish nationalists as a

'British' occasion, even though many thousands of Irish Catholics from North and South had fought with the British in both World Wars. The Cenotaph ceremonies were open to everyone, including Protestants, Roman Catholics and those of other religions or with no religion at all – but facts have little to do with perceptions in Ireland. There were, of course, a number of Catholic ex-Service men and women who took part in the Remembrance Day parades and ceremonies, and an unknown number of civilians who looked on. In recent years there has been evidence of greater cross-community participation, and Irish nationalist councillors in several parts of Northern Ireland have been present at such ceremonies – a development which has been noted and appreciated by the Unionist majority.

But old memories live longest, and Remembrance Day services were regarded primarily as a time for Unionists and Protestants to honour their dead. The Provisional IRA active service unit which planted its bomb in the building beside the Cenotaph would have been aware that the vast majority of the people gathered on that morning would have been Protestant civilians, as well as the security forces who were the alleged targets. There had been much evidence beforehand that primed bombs do not explode to order, or on time, and to plant a bomb in such a place at such a time was an act of monumental stupidity and savagery.

Ironically, Gordon was worried about security, as he approached the Cenotaph. It was not a premonition of what was to happen, but more the worry which many Ulster people have experienced throughout the Troubles of being in the wrong place at the wrong time – for example, when caught in traffic behind a security convoy which was a prime target for terrorists, or on such an occasion as a Remembrance Service where the presence of a large number of security forces would *de facto* make everyone a target. These were the kind of thoughts which crossed Gordon's mind as he prepared to take up position with Marie at the Cenotaph. He even mentioned to her that it looked very exposed and said, 'I sure hope the security forces made a good check last night.'

Gordon and Marie placed themselves where he stood every year. He always chose the old community building which provided shelter from winds and rain, and also afforded a good view of the ceremony, some

40 feet from the Cenotaph. It was in this building that the bomb had been planted, unknown to the security forces, and it was a wall of this building that was soon to engulf Gordon and Marie. With the benefit of hindsight, it seems incredible that a final sweep had not been taken of such a vulnerable area. Gordon, in his recollections, never once mentioned or criticized this lapse in security, but he told many an audience about the sensation of being caught up in a bomb explosion. Frequently he said, 'I went through a bomb', trying to convey to others what it really had meant, and the toll it had taken on his strength and resilience. In later years he talked about violence with such passion and compassion, and with such urgent fluency, that it was easy for others to take his searing, terrifying experience for granted. He described it graphically in these words:

'The "bang" was the first thing I heard. The thought went through my head, "My God, that's a bomb going off!" But this was a sharp sound, sharp enough to tell me that the bomb was not at the far end of town but very close. I don't know how anybody else was responding at that moment, but I turned as I stood, and I managed to look over my right shoulder. Marie was on my right. I must have realized that the bomb had gone off behind me, and I remember seeing the wall beginning to crack up. This all happened in a split second, but it seemed at the time as if everything was happening in slow motion, like a television replay.

'Then it seemed to me that I was pushed forward, and I came down on my face. This must have been happening very fast, but at the time it didn't seem at all like that. It was like being pushed down on my face in slow motion; it was extraordinary, really. Certainly, it was all happening, or seemed to be happening, slowly enough to give me time to think yet again, "My God, we're in a bomb blast! But it can't be! Not here – not at the Cenotaph on Remembrance Sunday!"

'At this point there was no sensation of noise that I can remember. There was no screaming, no shouting, but a kind of limitless, eerie silence. Having realized that the wall behind me was falling, I said to myself, "One big slab from that wall on the top of you, boy, and that'll be the end – that'll be it – it'll be goodbye!" But when the wall had finally finished collapsing, there was only the sound of debris trickling down after it. And my mind flashed through the message to my spread-eagled body, "The big one didn't get you after all!"

'By that stage I was flat on my face, and I must have been pushed on my mouth and nose, because my glasses had come off. I realized that we were buried beneath several feet of rubble, but there was a chink of light coming through, and I could feel the rainwater on the stones. I thought that my glasses had been lost. Normally I can see very little without them, but in the middle of all that I was able to see sufficiently well to spot the glasses and somehow to put them back on again, with one hand. It seemed like a miracle at the time.

'With my glasses I could also see some blood trickling down a stone, and I knew then that I was cut. I had been taking an anti-coagulant drug, and I was afraid that my blood would start to flow freely. As it happened, it was only a graze, and later the wound required only three or four stitches.

'All the time I was lying there on my mouth and nose, the noise level was increasing. Just after the blast there had been a sinister hush, a terrible quietness. And then the noise came, roaring and resounding and penetrating the several feet of rubble above us. There was shouting and moaning, and screaming, and yells of agony, until it all built up into a terrifying crescendo. At that stage a small voice inside me said, "I'm not too bad", and if that sounds like self-interest, it was also pure, basic human instinct, and a deep sense of thankfulness to be alive, even in a fix like that.'

In the midst of the blood, the hubbub and the screams of agony, Gordon's thoughts turned quickly to Marie. As they both lay under several feet of rubble, the events of the next few minutes were to inspire him, and also to haunt him, for the rest of his life:

'The explosion had thrown me forward, and my right arm was trapped. It later transpired that my shoulder had been dislocated, and therefore I had very little room for movement. At that point I realized that it was not possible to get out, certainly not without help from outside. But all through the screaming and shouting there was the urgent question in my mind: "Where's Marie? Is she hurt? Is she trapped? Is she alive?"

'Then, almost by magic, I found my hand being squeezed beneath that pile of rubble, and I knew it was Marie. She gripped my right hand and asked, "Is that you, Dad?" I could hardly believe that she was here, after all, lying beside me in the rubble. But the noise round about was increasing, so we had to shout louder and louder to make ourselves understood to each other. So we yelled, as best we could, amid the partial darkness and the noise.

'I shouted, "How are you, Marie?" She replied, "I'm fine." My heart skipped a beat with relief. But then, suddenly and terribly, she screamed. I knew that there must be something awfully wrong for her to scream like that. Again I asked her, "Are you all right?" And again came the reply, "Yes." But there seemed to be a bit of hesitation in that "Yes." A little later she shouted to me, "Dad, let's get out of here!" I replied, as best I could, "Marie, there's no getting out at the minute. We're trapped beneath all this rubble. But not to worry – they'll soon find us. There's a lot of people around, and they're certain to be digging down to us already. We've got enough air, there's a bit of light, and with God's help, we'll survive."

'But then she screamed again. I became desperately concerned about her condition. I could not, and I still cannot, understand how she could keep telling me that she was fine and yet, in between these messages of reassurance, she was screaming. Whether they were screams of pain or of terror I'll never know. I didn't know how badly she'd been hurt, but she was a very sensible girl of twenty, she had been trained as a nurse, and she would have known how to cope. She must have known she was hurt, and badly hurt. And I know now that she had been losing a great deal of blood by that stage.

'It must have been four or five times I shouted to Marie, "Are you all right?" But then, suddenly, her voice changed, and she sounded different. She held my hand tightly, and gripped me as hard as she could. She said, "Daddy, I love you very much." Those were her exact words to me, and those were the last words I ever heard her say. After that, her hand slipped away, and we lost touch.'

At this point Gordon fainted, lying face-down in the rubble, and he remembered gaining consciousness when the rescuers were trying to dig him out. He was covered in dirt and debris from the bomb-blast, and was unrecognizable to his rescuers. Two of them helped him towards a small parapet at the Cenotaph where he rested, while they went back to their daunting task of trying to pull more bodies, dead or alive, from the rubble. Gordon continued to fret about Marie, but noone could find her. More rescuers came to his aid, and he told them about the searing pain in his shoulder which, as medical staff found out later, had been dislocated in the explosion. Someone managed to get a wheelchair for Gordon, and he was taken to the casualty department of the local Erne Hospital, which was in the throes of a full-scale emergency.

Joan was in the kitchen of the family home at Cooper Crescent when the bomb went off. Peter had called in for a cup of coffee and had just left for church. The Wilsons' house sits high on a hill about a mile from the Cenotaph, and the sound of the bomb was heard for miles around. For so many people in Northern Ireland the sound of a bomb going off was a depressing and demoralizing experience, because they knew that it would mean more death, misery, suffering and destruction. Such a sound, however, was not always the dramatic roar of an explosion at close quarters, as portrayed on television or in the cinema; rather, it was often a dull, distant thud. That's how the Enniskillen bomb sounded to Joan as she cleared up the coffee cups before preparing to set off for church. She wondered whether the thud had been the noise of Peter banging his car door loudly or whether it had been a bomb.

Within a few minutes, however, Peter returned. It had indeed been a bomb which had gone off at the Cenotaph, and Peter and Joan both knew that Gordon and Marie were in the crowd of bystanders at the Remembrance Day ceremony. They were both frightened, and so set off to find out what had happened. Before doing so, Joan phoned Julie Anne and told her that a bomb had gone off at the Cenotaph. Julie Anne had also heard the explosion when she had left her house earlier to buy some milk at a local shop on her way to church. She also made for the centre of the town. She recalls: 'There was an awful panic everywhere. I was aware that Dad and Marie had been at the Cenotaph, and I had this dreadful fear that they were lost. People were running about in the midst of chaos, and I knew many of them personally. I stayed around for what seemed a long time, but in reality it was only about half an hour. By this stage people were not looking at me straight in the eye, and that made me think that something terrible was wrong with Dad and Marie. I set off to meet up with Mum. It was dreadful.'

Meanwhile, Joan had waited in a car-park with baby Judith, while Peter tried to find out more information, without success. They decided to return to the family home, in case Gordon and Marie had gone there. But no one was at Cooper Crescent when they arrived back, nor did the phone ring. So they decided to go to the Methodist Church in Darling Street, but Gordon and Marie were not there either. Though Joan was becoming alarmed by this stage, she never dreamt that they would have been directly caught up in the bomb. While at the church, Joan went into the Sunday school to talk to her daughter-in-law Ingrid, who had not heard or heard about the explosion. Then Julie Anne arrived at the church, and she and Peter decided to make their way to the Erne Hospital, to see whether they could glean any news there.

The scene was one of pandemonium. Casualties were being wheeled in, medical staff on duty were in the midst of emergency procedures, off-duty staff who had heard the explosion or reports about the carnage were rushing in to help. Groups of shocked and tearful relatives were waiting for snippets of news, while friends and local clergy were trying to provide as much support and comfort as they could. Gordon was moved from Casualty to a Physiotherapy Room, which was being used as a clearing station. His physical pain was intense, but even after the doctors had put back his dislocated shoulder, his mental anguish continued unabated. Still there was no news whatever of Marie.

The Archbishop of Armagh, Dr Robin Eames (now Lord Eames), was with other clergy in the hospital. He had been due to preach at the Cathedral that morning. He recounts some of the details of what was then taking place:

> I will never forget that day as long as I live. The scene at the hospital was unbelievable. Ambulances and private cars bringing the injured, relatives rushing in looking for news, off-duty staff arriving to help those on duty, frantic searching for news, people covered in

dust, many of them bleeding – but above all this shock and disbe-lief, a hospital responding magnificently to the emergency.

I was joined by Bishop Hannon, and we began to talk to people and to do what we could to comfort the distressed. Lying on a trolley in one room was Gordon Wilson. We had met before at an ecumenical occasion, but although we did not really know each other well, I recognized him immediately. He told me something of what had happened. Then came the question that was to haunt us all that day: 'Do you know anything about Marie?' I did not, but quickly said, 'We'll try to find out.' The corridors and rooms were full of the injured, their relatives, army and police, and natu-rally there was considerable confusion. During the early afternoon I was talking to some medical staff, and the question arose about identifying a girl who had been admitted for surgery. The tragedy was then plain for all to see. Father and daughter had been sepa-rated by a few yards of corridor, and because of the difficulties of identification the two were not linked.

For Gordon and his family those hours in the Erne Hospital were a nightmare. In the confusion many, many personal dramas were being played out. None could match the irony or pathos of the search for Marie. No one was to blame for the failure to link the two – such was the confusion in the corridors of the hospital. Gordon's question remains with me as it will always – 'Do you know anything about Marie?'

My vivid memory remains of a human tragedy, being met by the dedicated hearts and minds of the staff – and the frantic search for loved ones. It was in that scenario that Gordon Wilson's per-sonal tragedy was beginning to appear for the outside world.

Meanwhile, Joan had decided initially to stay at the church. She had talked to several very distressed youngsters from the Girls' Brigade who had been at the Cenotaph, and her anxieties multiplied. The minister, Tom Magowan, asked her if she wanted to sit quietly in the body of the church, but she chose to play the organ for the service, reasoning to her-self that she would prefer to be occupied rather than sitting alone and anticipating the worst. But after some twenty minutes she could not go on. Then a member of the Ulster Defence Association, who was also a church member, arrived and beckoned to her. He told her that Gordon was in the hospital with a broken arm. She asked him, 'What about Marie? Has anyone found Marie?' But he replied, 'I wouldn't know about that.' Joan felt herself thinking, quite sharply, 'And why not?' Her anxiety and fear were increasing by the minute.

Peter had come back to drive his mother to the hospital. He told her that Gordon was there with a broken arm, but there was no sign of Marie. Joan began to cry and to fear the worst for Marie. They reached the hospital around mid-day, more than an hour after the explosion took place, and they spent the next few hours in the agony of waiting. Joan was taken to Gordon, who by now was sitting in a wheelchair with his arm dislocated and with a cut on his forehead. Gordon's first words to her, as to anyone within hearing distance during those awful hours, were 'Any news of Marie?' Then he broke down and said, 'The pet told me she loved me!' Gordon often referred to Marie as 'the pet', but Joan did not immediately pick up the significance of what he was saying. Only slowly was she able to piece together the complex story of what had happened only an hour earlier. To her horror she realized that a wall had fallen on them due to the force of the explosion, and that they had been buried under rubble. She also heard that a local man, Johnny Megaw, whom she knew well, had been killed, and that another couple, Nessie and Billy Mullan, were missing. She could not believe what was happening.

Gordon was taken for an X-ray, and doctors put his shoulder back in place and gave him a pain-killing injection. He was wheeled back to the holding area, and Joan sat by his bed. It was not until 2.30 p.m. that Peter and Julie Anne were able to discover from a policeman that Marie was being operated upon in theatre. Julie Anne takes up the story: 'When I came into the hospital, I found Dad lying on the bed. He looked dishevelled, with dust all over his hair, and covered in grime from the rubble. He was in pain, but talking sense. We were all up the walls about Marie, and Dad kept asking about her again and again. After a while we tried to change the subject, but he kept coming back to the same question: 'Where's Marie? What about Marie?' Mum was very strong, very calm, just when we needed her. Some people were crying, others seemed to be taking things in their stride. There were so many different stories, and I began to get a bit impatient, even cross. No one seemed to be able to tell us what was going on. Then news came that someone was in theatre – a young girl. Someone asked, "Does anybody know a young woman who was wearing a pink dress and blue tights?" That was Marie! Then someone else brought us jewellery to help with the identification. It was Marie's watch, and her bracelet which had been dented by the impact of the bomb. I still have her bracelet upstairs in my home, and it is one of my most treasured possessions. At about 2.40 p.m. one of the doctors came to talk to us all. He didn't beat about the bush. Marie was suffering from severe brain damage.'

Gordon asked the doctor, 'Sir, are you telling us there's no hope for Marie?' He replied, 'We're fighting for her life and we're still hoping.' Joan noticed a forlorn poppy lying on the floor under a bed. It symbolized to her the suffering, the disorder, the total mayhem.

Ten minutes later, another doctor and a nursing officer asked Joan, Peter and Julie Anne into a small office nearby. The family were preparing for the worst. As well as the severe brain damage, Marie's young body was wracked with serious injuries. She had had a cardiac arrest when she was brought to the hospital. Her pelvis was broken, she had internal injuries and she was bleeding profusely. Already the doctors had given her 24 pints of blood. A nursing officer arrived to tell them that Marie was now out of theatre and in Intensive Care. Gordon was told the distressing news. He was still lying in bed, in pain, and he was not fit enough to accompany the others to the Intensive Care Ward upstairs. On the way up, a lady doctor whose daughter had died of cancer some months earlier at the age of 27, took Joan in her arms and whispered words of comfort: 'Please God, you won't lose your dear daughter too.'

Julie Anne stood beside her mother in Intensive Care, watching as Marie's life slipped away. 'Her hair was dusty, the place seemed full of tubes. It was terrible. Marie didn't look like herself at all. I had this horrific feeling, and the minute I saw her a voice welled up in me saying,

"Please, let her die – she wouldn't want it this way!" If there was any question of keeping her alive, I just did not want her to be like that, and I knew deep in my heart that she would not have wanted that either.'

Joan remembers her daughter's last moments: 'I kissed her gently. Her face looked so different. There were scratches on her cheek. The Ward Sister told us that Marie's heart was still beating, but that it could stop at any minute. The doctor who had fought so valiantly with the others to save her life was standing by the bed. He just looked at us and shook his head sadly. I am sure that Marie could hear our voices. I saw her eyelids flutter, and I will remember that to my dying day. Then the Ward Sister said to us gently, "Marie's heart has stopped beating. It's all over." Our darling Marie – the girl so full of life and vitality – was no more. I was in a state of total disbelief. Julie Anne took my hand and said, "Mum, it's better this way." I could only utter the prayer, "The Lord gave, the Lord has taken away. Blessed be the name of the Lord." I knew that I had to lean hard on the Lord now – he was my only strength. I had to go down and tell Gordon that his darling daughter was dead. I kept going back to look at Marie. I am sure that I walked in and out of that little room six times or more, until Sister gently reminded me that I had a duty to go downstairs and to tell Gordon.'

The three devastated figures – Joan, Peter and Julie Anne – made their way down the stairs. Julie Anne said later: 'I could not bear to stay in that room. I remember going out, embracing Mum and finally closing the door. That was my way. Different people have different ways of coping. When we got downstairs, Mum told Dad the awful news. She put her arms around him gently and said, "Our child is dead." He cried out, "Oh, my God, is Marie dead?" I remember going over to him and holding his hand. No words were uttered. He just could not speak at all. When we got home, I remember making him scrambled eggs, but food didn't matter. I kept thinking of him leaving our house that morning with Marie beside him, and coming back that evening without her, and Marie lying dead in the hospital down the road. It was just too terrible for words.'

Joan remembers the forlorn journey back home. Tom Magowan wheeled Gordon to Peter's car. 'Gordon was lamenting deeply, between his pain and his distress. But I recall him saying all that had to be said, as he so often had done. He said, "Life has to go on. It is going to be different for us all, from now on. The next few days will be particularly difficult, but let's stick together as a family, and let's try, with God's help, to muster as much strength and dignity as we can."'

Already the news of the carnage at the Cenotaph was making headlines around the world. The news teams had been in Enniskillen since mid-day, and it was only a matter of time before they would make their way to the Wilsons' door. The Enniskillen bomb had shattered the heart of their family that day, but the coming hours would also intrude upon their private grief and thrust Gordon into the world's spotlight.

Meanwhile Marie lay dead in the hospital mortuary, just five months short of her twenty-first birthday. Her tragic involvement in the Enniskillen carnage was over, and her voice was silenced. But her last words would live on to touch the hearts of so many people and to inspire her father and others to unimagined depths of forgiveness and strength. Her death, though brutal and still unbearably moving in the telling, would not be in vain.

5

Under the Spotlight

When the family returned to Cooper Crescent, the house was dark and silent, but within minutes of their arrival the phone and the door-bell started to ring almost incessantly. News of the Enniskillen carnage had spread quickly, and people from near and far were anxious to pay their respects to the families of all those who had died, and to those who were injured. Ulster society is well known for its care and comfort during bereavement, and neighbours and friends rally round quickly. So it was with the Wilsons. In all, eleven people had been killed (some of the relatives would say 'murdered', but the Wilson family have never used that expression). Those who died were Samuel Gault, a retired policeman; Kit Johnston, an ambulance driver, and his wife Jessie; William Mullan, a chemist, and his wife Nessie; Wesley Armstrong, a BT employee, and his wife Bertha; Edward Armstrong (no relation), a reserve policeman; Johnny Megaw, a local handyman who was well known and appreciated for his hospital visits to the elderly; Georgina Quinton, a retired nursing sister; and Marie Wilson. More than 60 people were injured, including local primary school principal Ronnie Hill, who has remained in a coma ever since. The total devotion of his wife Noreen and family has been one of the most poignant yet noble and inspiring stories of the entire Troubles.

Each of the Enniskillen families has its own story of sorrow and courage to tell, and it was a complex combination of circumstances that conspired to thrust Gordon Wilson into the world's spotlight. This was something he felt deeply, and he was ever at pains to point out that he was not the only victim of the Enniskillen bomb, nor did he pretend to speak for the others, or indeed for the thousands of victims of the long nightmare of the Troubles. His suffering was symbolic of the unending trauma of Northern Ireland, but he always said, 'I speak only on behalf of Marie Wilson and her family.'

The challenge of facing the media began almost immediately. From early evening, the Wilson household was crowded with people. Friends and neighbours took over the kitchen, and sandwiches, cakes and tea appeared as if by magic for the large number of visitors, some of whom were now queuing outside the front gate. In traditional country style, everything was being taken care of with dignity and respect. Gordon and Joan shared their grief with many on that night, but there was opportunity to say only a few words. There were very few tears, partly because of the sense of deep shock felt by everyone, and most of all by the family. The enormity of the suffering was such, not only in the Wilson home but in ten other homes in Enniskillen, that people did not know what to say, or how to say it. As Gordon often used to remark after visiting others who had been bereaved, 'There's nothing you can put into words. A strong, sympathetic handshake says it all.'

Julie Anne had her own way of trying to cope with the devastating, wrenching loss of her only sister: 'I remember going up to Marie's bedroom, sitting on her bed and sorting out her personal things. That was hard, because I wanted to share this with my Mum and Dad, and not to face the world downstairs. I didn't want to go from room to room meeting people whom I did not know. Peter and Ingrid had each other. My friends at that time were very, very supportive, and that was good, but most of all I needed my parents. I understood that they were doing what they had to do, and I did not blame them for not devoting all their attention to me.'

She was aching with the pain of losing Marie and did not know how to handle it. 'I was trying to cope as best I could, but I really resented the media coming. Our private grief, which was not at that stage private anyway, would be exposed to the whole world. But Dad was the opposite, and I also understood and respected his reasons for talking to the reporters. But it was not easy. My natural instinct was to close the door on all of them.'

Among the stream of callers at the door that night was the reporter who first brought Gordon Wilson's unforgettable words to the outside

world, Mike Gaston, a freelance radio journalist. He had first heard of
the explosion when a duty editor from Associated Press Radio in Wash-
ington phoned him in Belfast at eleven in the morning about a news-
flash from Enniskillen. As the AP 'stringer' for Ireland, he was quickly
on the move, and told the duty editor for BBC Radio Ulster that he was
heading for Enniskillen. Now the Managing Director of Belfast Community Radio, he recalls the events of that day:

> A thousand years ago yesterday...I was in Enniskillen on the edge
> of a story like no other. Of course, every story is like no other, but
> this one was really different. I'd arrived at Enniskillen by mid-day,
> and I'd done the preliminary eyewitness interviews – a rescue
> worker, a butcher's apprentice, a Bishop and, in common with the
> rest of the world's press, I was camped out at the Erne Hospital.
> Mick Breslin, the Editor of the *Fermanagh Herald*, recognized my
> voice and offered help. His wasn't the only offer of help – just the
> most significant. Amongst the people he introduced me to was
> Peter Wilson, waiting to collect his father who had been injured
> by the bomb. Peter didn't want to be interviewed, so we arranged
> a meeting with his father for later that evening.
>
> Meanwhile there was much to do. Like hearing the Reverend
> David Cupples, a young minister recently appointed to Enniskil-
> len, battle through his tears to tell his congregation that six of
> their best-loved members were dead. And the medical staff coping
> with their own sense of grief as they tended former colleagues and
> friends. And the survivors describing the crushing terror of the
> bomb. The pain, the shock, the sorrow, the kindness and the lack
> of anger were getting past my normal defences.
>
> I had already contacted a BBC colleague, Charlie Warmington,
> an Enniskillen man who knew Gordon Wilson, and after the ser-
> vice in the Enniskillen Church, I went with Charlie to the Wilson
> home where he introduced me to Gordon. I was made to feel wel-
> come – rather than as a professional vulture, which is how I usually
> felt. I empathized acutely with Gordon. One of my daughters was
> ill, my mother was dying. I was aching with fear, dread and love for

them both. And here was Gordon, whose much-loved daughter had been crushed to death. He almost unwillingly lived on with the gut-wrenching guilt of survival and the searing pain of loss.

We spoke a little and shared much more. Then I asked him to tell me what happened in his own words. And I've never ever heard anything like it before...and I never will again:

'As we crossed the bridge just beside where the bomb went off – and ten minutes before it did – I said to Marie "I hope the police have checked that bridge – that's a very open target." We walked back and we just positioned ourselves with our backs to the wall that collapsed, the wall of the house or hall or school.

'And ten seconds later we were both thrown forward. Rubble and stones and whatever in and round and over us and under us. I remember thinking "I'm not hurt." Then I was aware of a pain in my right shoulder. I shouted to Marie was she all right and she said "Yes" and she found my hand and said, "Is that your hand, Dad?"

'Now remember we were under six foot of rubble. I said, "Are you all right?" and she said, "Yes", but she was shouting in between. Three or four times I asked her and she always said, "Yes", she was all right.

'When I asked her the fifth time..."Are you all right, Marie?" ...she said..."Daddy I love you very much."...Those were the last words she spoke to me. She still held my hand quite firmly and I kept shouting at her, "Marie, are you all right?"...There wasn't a reply.

'We were there about five minutes. Someone came and pulled me out. I said, "I'm all right...but for God's sake my daughter is lying right beside me...and I don't think she's too well..."
'She's dead...She didn't die there...She died later.

'The hospital was magnificent, truly impressive, and our friends have been great, but I have lost my daughter, and we shall miss her. But I bear no ill will, I bear no grudge. Dirty sort of talk is not going to bring her back to life. She was a great wee lassie. She loved her profession. She was a pet and she's dead. She's in Heaven, and we'll meet again. Don't ask me, please, for a purpose. I *don't have a purpose. I don't have an answer. But I know there has to be a plan. If I didn't think that, I would commit suicide. It's part of a greater plan, and God is good. And we shall meet again.'*

Tears almost swamping me, I climbed into the car to feed the tape to Belfast. The studio crew had heard it all before. It was just a job to them, as it usually was to me. But with this most unusual story this otherwise ordinary, decent, middle-aged man managed to reduce them to tears. And almost everyone else who heard him.

The interview was recorded in a 'straight take', after a short preliminary conversation to establish the sound quality. Gaston said later: 'I did not dare interrupt him because I realized, as the interview progressed, that it was one of the most remarkable pieces of broadcasting I had heard in 30 years. Gordon, being Gordon, told it as it was, just as he felt it. He had absolutely no idea of the impact it would have, but I knew that it was of historic magnitude, and utterly unique. The next day Gordon talked to the television crews, and they came from all over the place. I told some of his friends to try to dissuade him from torturing himself in this way, because I knew that he would be approached by everyone, from Nippon TV to the *Outer Mongolia Times*.'

Mike did not exaggerate. Gordon's initial broadcast on radio was heart-stopping, throbbing with pain, and totally unforgettable. It was an authentic voice from the deepest abyss of suffering and pain, and yet it had a miraculous quality of spiritual strength and a total lack of ill-will. Those who heard it live will always remember that moment when a man's private grief touched the raw nerve of human vulnerability that lies deep in all of us and brought forth a huge wave of compassion from every heart. It will be remembered as one of the major turning-points in people's attitudes to the sad and bloody history of the island of Ireland, not because of any political or social developments it engendered directly, but because it exposed in its raw nakedness the agony of human pain and the futility of violence. In a deep sense, the culture of violence was discredited for ever, and even though violence continued afterwards, Enniskillen posed a question mark about the past, and a challenge to work for a better future for all.

Was Gordon aware of any of this as he gave the interview? He recalled later: 'When the BBC reporter asked me to say a few words that night, I was unaware of the extent of the shock-waves that were going out from Enniskillen. He was very courteous, and after one or two "warming up" remarks, I answered his request, "Tell me what happened this morning." As best I could, I described the events at the Cenotaph, and I talked about lying under the rubble with Marie, and her squeezing my hand, and of her last words to me: "Daddy, I love you very much."

'Mike Gaston had asked me a question, and I had given him a straight answer. That night the interview was broadcast, and the next morning as well. Personally I had no inkling whatever of the effect it would have.'

Several days after the bomb, Mike Gaston tried to explain to his young daughter why it had all happened. He remembers: 'I couldn't of course, but I tried anyway, and it seemed to help us for a time. I'll never ever forget, and every time someone asks me to talk about Enniskillen and Gordon's interview, a lump comes to my throat. In some ways I wish he had never talked to me, not because of the impact it had on people, but because of what that good, vulnerable and gentle man brought upon himself. If he had not been thrust into the limelight, his life would have been more peaceful afterwards. Years later, I wrote a poem called "The Reporter" about a day I'll never forget.'

Here is Mike's poem:

You brought me to your fireside
Like a neighbour
Sitting with your family
I felt the total disbelief
The utter desolation

Your friends were wonderful
As they tried to share
Pain beyond bearing
Their words of comfort
For themselves as much as you

'She was a great girl
So full of life.'
You nod almost unhearing

'She was his wee favourite, you know'
As if your other two
Were quite beyond hurt

'She was planning her twenty-first,
It would have been a rare do.'

I sat transfixed
The rip in your trouser leg
A grim reminder
Of blasted crushing stone

'Would you like a cup of tea?'
Jaws move mechanically
Glad of the ritual

The undertaker comes
To make hushed arrangements
In the hall outside.

I want to escape
From my bloody trade
'We have to speak' I say
Sounding braver than I feel
Unbidden the room clears

Then there's your voice
The finest distillation
Of the bardic tradition
Like High Kings never heard

Your phrases would move
The stones that crushed her
But will they touch
Hard hearts of rock

You tell me her last words
Were words of love
And then you say
'Bitter words won't bring her back'
Nor will they.

But

Your grief, your love, your courage
Made death-dealers stand still
And saved lives and changed lives
For a little while

And cost you very dear
We listened too hard
For hope we lacked
And missed the point.

Gordon's memorable broadcast literally brought the world's media to the door. In the days before the funeral, Gordon gave interviews from early in the morning until late in the afternoon. The pressure became so great that Julie Anne told him, 'For God's sake, Dad, tell them to go. Surely you've had enough!' Several years later, Gordon reflected on those hectic hours and explained exactly why he had talked to the media:

> There was no way I could not talk, having given the initial broadcast, and I had no thoughts to the contrary. The fact of suffering was there for all to see. Some people had reacted to my radio broadcast and had said, 'He's in a state of shock. He can't mean

what he says!' Even though I was indeed shocked, and although my voice had broken with emotion once or twice during the broadcast, I knew exactly what I was saying. And I would like to think that if the same thing happened again, I would have the grace to use the same words.

Some people have since asked me, 'How did you endure such pressure? Where did you find the energy to keep on talking? Did you feel any kind of purpose in talking to so many media people, or were you rather dazed by it all and carried along on their tide of questions?' The answer is simple. I gave the first couple of interviews because I was trying to be courteous and I did not want to turn people away. I lacked experience with the media, and I thought that each interview would be the last. But when you have talked to one or two reporters you cannot in all fairness refuse the others. Of course I was tired, and throughout that day one part of me was saying, 'This is all going too far.' But another part of me was thinking that the bombing was so horrible that people should be told about it, at first hand. Perhaps subconsciously I was also saying that if sufficient people were shocked by what happened in Enniskillen, this might help to make them say 'Enough is enough', and to begin to bring this country to its senses. While at no time, then or since, did I regard myself as a 'spokesman' for Enniskillen, I moved from being merely courteous to realizing that this story had to be told. Even though friends and family were advising me to ease off, I felt that my interviews were achieving an important purpose. At no point was I 'dazed' or 'carried along' on the tide of questions. At all times I was in total control and I felt that the story should be told as simply and as lucidly as possible. Some of the media portrayed me as 'The Voice of Enniskillen', but that was not my doing. I saw myself as *a* voice but not *the* voice of Enniskillen.

It is important to emphasize that Gordon's initial broadcast, on the night of Marie's death, was entirely his own. There had not been an opportunity, or even an inclination, to hold a family discussion in order to present an agreed statement. In that context Gordon was his own person, though he had the broad support of his family. Julie Anne recalls: 'I was proud of him. What he said was completely from the heart, but after the first couple of interviews I wish he had left it at that. He became completely wrapped up in the media, because he really believed that what he was saying would make a difference to the situation in Northern Ireland. I understand why he felt he had to do it, and despite the trauma and the suffering, a great deal of what happened later on with the media was good for him. It took him out of himself, it was a form of therapy, but also it took him away from me. And I found that hard.'

Joan reflects: 'I don't know how he did it. On the night of Marie's death he was in great pain and distress, yet he was able to sit there and say what he said. It was amazing. He had been at the centre of raw, naked terror, and yet he was able to say the right thing, so powerfully and so beautifully. If he had shown hatred or anger in that broadcast, or subsequent broadcasts, there might have been a terrible backlash from the Loyalists. Feelings at that time were running very high. I had never been in such a state. When our baby son Richard died, we were very cut up. Gordon cried a great deal about that, but the bomb was the biggest calamity of our lives, and he was facing it in his way.'

Joan was facing it in her way too. Initially she would not have been nearly as compassionate as Gordon. Her gut reaction was one of passionate anger:

How could they do that to so many innocent human beings? How could they live with themselves? How could they look at themselves in the mirror after committing such unspeakably savage crimes? Even today, when I think of what they did to Ronnie Hill, who has lain in a coma ever since, and what they have done to his wife Noreen and the rest of the family, I can still feel stabs of anger coming back. My initial and deep anger at Marie's death did not go away easily or quickly. It lasted all through the funeral, and for many months afterwards. I had to work at overcoming it. Gordon's words were a great help, because I knew deep down that he was right.

I realized that anger and bitterness are not good. They eat you up and you could become very bitter yourself. I understand, very well, how people could be caught up in bitterness and anger at such awful crimes. In my case, I prayed that out of all this rubble and chaos, some good might come. I was very feeble, but I believed deeply that God would work something positive from this deep darkness and destruction. We were really up against it, as a family, and what else could we do? I had been trained all my life to ask for God's help, and I did so. The Lord did not fail me in the crises.

Looking back, I still think sometimes that it's all a bad dream. I will never really get over Marie's death. I have learned how to pace myself, but even now I find myself thinking of what Marie might be doing, if she were alive. Would she be married, would she have children, where would she be nursing? And even today I have to keep clear in my mind Marie's last words of love, and Gordon's words of forgiveness. I still pray for the bombers, every night. I say a simple prayer: 'Lord, grant that those who planted the bomb will repent, and come to know your forgiveness.' That is all I can do, but I think it is important to keep these people in my prayers. I always felt that Gordon was spared from that terrible blast for some special reason. God was in the situation with him, and in retrospect I now see why he was spared. He did help the overall situation in his own way by doing what he did. I could not have done that. My role was to comfort him and support him to the best of my ability, and in that way to help him to do what was laid out before him.

On the night Marie died, Gordon was in no fit state physically to begin that arduous mission of reconciliation and forgiveness which was to inspire, absorb and so often utterly exhaust him in the years to come. He was sitting at home, a physically shattered man being ministered to by his family and closest friends. But already his words were being relayed to a world which, in the long saga of suffering in Northern Ireland, had never heard anything quite like it. Lord Eames, who in common with far too many ministers in Northern Ireland, had had to find words of comfort, hope and courage for the bereaved on all sides, heard Gordon's broadcast and was deeply moved. He recalls: 'I shared the overwhelming reaction of people who were astounded by his capacity to forgive. I prayed that in time, and given the prevailing atmosphere of suspicion and division, that those words would not be manipulated for political or sectarian reasons. Personally, I felt that they were the words of a true Christian whose courage and faith many would envy. I greatly admired his courage, but also realized that unless you faced *that* situation yourself, you did not have any right to make a judgement. His words gave me great hope, and I felt they would become historic.'

Alan Hanna, who had known Gordon and the Wilson family as their minister and pastor, said later: 'I was in no way surprised at Gordon's words, but equally I would not have been surprised if some time later there had been a reaction. It was wonderful how his message reached the world, and has been an inspiration to so many. I would like to see his attitude, his words, his influence highlighted more and more – but as a man who represented so many others on both sides, who have shown the same spirit, and who live to help heal the wounds. And I also have a sneaking sympathy for those who suffer and who suffer on terribly, because they cannot forgive or throw resentment and bitterness overboard.'

In Dublin, Father Brian D'Arcy, who had known Gordon as the big, gangly Protestant shopkeeper who always had a friendly word for a passing Catholic schoolboy, heard the news of the Enniskillen explosion, and he was distraught. When he heard Gordon's words he thought again of the large man from Enniskillen holding out his big hands of forgiveness to all the world, and he wept.

David Bolton, a social worker, was at the hospital within minutes of the bombing and later worked, with others, to support the victims and their families. He believes that Gordon could not have anticipated the response his interview would generate: 'His words were a father's words, for a daughter who had died so tragically. They resonated with the hearts of any who have known a parent's love or the love for a child. When I hear that interview, even now, I find my heart stirred, a lump rises in my throat, and my eyes sting as the tears well up. It was, and is, a most powerful, moving expression of human experience.'

The bombing, he feels, was such an outrage that the broader Nationalist community, North and South, were deeply hurt and ashamed that this event had come from their community. 'The bombing effectively separated the two communities and threatened to disconnect the Catholic community from the natural expression of its sorrow and support. If eleven people had died by some other means than a political act, then the matter of Protestant or Catholic would hardly have been visible at all, and both communities would have readily engaged in supporting the other, and, importantly, in accepting that support.' Gordon's interview accentuated the awfulness of what had happened in that he spoke so movingly of the dying of Marie, and at the same time, through his generosity, he opened up the means by which the Catholic community could re-engage in sharing and acknowledging the sorrow of their Protestant and Unionist neighbours.

In a sense, David Bolton believes, Gordon's contribution was both timely and untimely. It was timely because, at a political level, it reduced the risks of terrible reprisals. The awfulness of what had happened as described by him (and others who spoke out at the time) was so great that the loss and suffering pushed the political differences into the background.

On the other hand, at an emotional level, his words were untimely, and it was for this reason that he attracted criticism. 'I have no doubt that he meant what he said. He was that sort of man; he said what he meant. But others did not feel the things he was feeling. It was not that they felt angry or revengeful. Rather, most of us did not know what to think, or feel, so close to the bombing. I remember on the evening of the bombing thinking I should feel angry. But all I could feel was nothing, and was aware that we were all caught up in a terrible drama.'

Gordon gave expression to views and thoughts which many, and probably most, could not recognize in themselves. Many were responding to a gut feeling, probably in part influenced by the political circumstances. This was a political act and demanded a political (even an emotionally political) response. Gordon said what he said on principle.

He could not have said anything else. It was a Christ-like response. He heaped coals on the heads of those responsible for the bombing.

Looking back, his words were simple, plain and innocuous. He said he bore Marie's killers 'no ill will'. Those words, caught up in the editorial and headline mechanisms of newspapers and broadcasting organizations, were re-interpreted as 'forgiveness'. This extension of the meaning and intention of Gordon's statement led to Gordon, his family, and others who had been bereaved and injured, and even Enniskillen itself, being turned into objects of inspiration, which left little room for the natural expression of outrage and sorrow. David Bolton comments: 'Gordon was locked into a media role. Enniskillen was locked into a straightjacket, a situation which I, along with others, sought to reverse, to give people room to feel what they were feeling and not what the media or the country wanted us to feel.'

The media reaction was indeed overwhelming, as writers, reporters and editors tried to find words to capture the depth of popular feeling for this extraordinary man, Gordon Wilson, and for what he represented. The *Sunday Times* wrote: 'Mr Wilson, for one, has generated much hope that good may yet come from Marie's untimely and brutal death.' The local Enniskillen paper, *The Impartial Reporter*, referred to Gordon as 'one bright light across the globe...a man of unshakeable faith'. However, there were other people who did not share the views of Gordon Wilson. They felt that he had been wrong in what he had said, that he had no right to forgive terrorists, that he was naive and out of his depth.

Comment and analysis and even criticism would flow for weeks to come, but on the night of Marie's death, after all the visitors and reporters had gone, the shattered family finally got to bed, but they could not sleep. It was the longest night of their lives. They tried to talk, but had few words to offer each other. They walked about the house, upstairs and downstairs. Gordon and Joan held hands and bodies, as they sobbed and cried. They grieved their loss with hours of uncontrollable agony. It seemed as though the dawn would never come. Silently they prayed again and again for others and for themselves, that God would give them the strength and the grace to meet the days ahead.

6

Grief – Public and Private

Detailed and probing media coverage of the Enniskillen bomb continued relentlessly throughout the next few days. Everything about the Remembrance Day horror was covered, and Gordon's broadcasts produced an immediate effect. A senior Tory backbencher told a reporter: 'I'm not ashamed to say it, there were tears in my eyes when I heard his words. It really was a day of infamy.' Joan remembers that among the thousands of letters of sympathy which the family began to receive, there were a number from people from all over Great Britain and the Irish Republic and elsewhere, including Saudi Arabia, Canada, America, Austria, India and the Philippines. All these people had heard Gordon's words about Marie. Joan recalls: 'People told me they heard it while driving to work, and they had to pull in to a lay-by. They could not drive because of their tears. Housewives told me that when they heard it, they sat down at the kitchen table and cried.'

On that Sunday afternoon, the Queen led the nation in mourning and issued a statement outlining her deep shock at what she described as 'the Enniskillen atrocity'. She offered her 'heartfelt sympathy…to the bereaved and injured in their distress'. Pope John Paul II also expressed his 'profound shock'.

The American President Ronald Reagan spoke of the 'revulsion' of the American people and stated in a letter of condolence to the then British Prime Minister, Margaret Thatcher, 'It is a very cruel irony that such a deed should be done on a day of remembrance.' Mrs Thatcher, who was visibly moved by the suffering, also alluded to the especially evil nature of the bombing which took place at a Cenotaph. She said: 'Every civilized nation honours and respects its dead. To take advantage of the people assembled in that way was really a desecration. It was so cruel, so callous, that the people who did it can have no human thoughtfulness or kindness or sensitivity at all. It was utterly barbaric.'

Seamus Mallon, the Deputy Leader of the mainly Roman Catholic Social Democratic and Labour Party, bitterly condemned the bombing. He said: 'It was sacrilegious in that people were killed as they remembered and prayed for their dead. It was obviously sectarian because those who planted the bomb knew that the vast majority of people at the service would be of the Protestant faith.' The Irish Prime Minister, Charles Haughey, said: 'I know that I speak for every decent Irish man and Irish woman in expressing the anger and revulsion we feel towards those who planned and executed this criminal act of carnage against the innocent people gathered to commemorate their dead.'

The Irish Prime Minister's words were prophetic. In the Republic there was a very marked and widespread reaction of horror, anger and revulsion at this barbaric act, which had been perpetrated, ostensibly, for the cause of a united Ireland. The Wilson family received letters from every corner of Ireland, and the people of the Republic took Gordon to their hearts, particularly when he became a Member of the Irish Senate. In the overwhelming deluge of tributes and messages of condolence, two acts of sympathy from the Republic stood out. On the Sunday after the bombing, there was a one-minute silence throughout the Republic, after which the Lord Mayor of Dublin, Carmencita Hederman, who was in Enniskillen, presented a Book of Condolences from the people of the Republic. Instead of making her carefully prepared speech, she broke down in tears. Gordon said afterwards: 'That very act of breaking down told us more of her heartfelt sympathy and solidarity, and that of the many people she represented, than a thousand well-turned phrases.' The other touching gesture from the Republic was the presentation of a large salmon by Protestant and Roman Catholic members of a West of Ireland fishing village. The gift symbolized their cross-community solidarity as well as their livelihood.

Even today, it is difficult to understand fully the reasons for the overwhelming impact of the Enniskillen explosion. There had been many bad days in the history of Northern Ireland, when innocent people on both sides had been mown down by gunfire, or blown apart by an explosion. Perhaps Enniskillen was different because the violence was indeed seen as sacrilegious, in that innocent people were killed in the very act of honouring their dead. It was as if violence had intruded upon holy ground, upon the territory which people on all sides, including (it had been thought) the people of violence, regarded as out of bounds. Enniskillen showed that the hitherto sacred act of honouring the dead was no longer immune. This touched a nerve in people throughout the world, and created a unique kind of revulsion. Even the Soviet official news agency Tass, which was not known for its sympathy to the British in Northern Ireland, described the explosion as a 'barbaric act'. In a direct way, Gordon Wilson gave that act of barbarity a flesh-and-blood dimension, as he showed the face of a distressed and deeply grieving parent with whom everyone could identify. It was a powerful combination of universal horror and individual suffering that would leave an indelible mark.

The newspaper headlines told the story starkly and simply: 'No mercy by the callous killers'; 'We should have been paying tribute to our dead, not digging them out'. People on every side were quick to condemn the bombing, apart from Sinn Fein, the political wing of the Republican movement. Paul Corrigan, the Sinn Fein chairman of Fermanagh District Council, was quoted as 'regretting' the 'tragic loss of life', but deliberately avoided blaming the IRA. He had 'grave doubts' whether the Provisionals were responsible. He told a reporter: 'I wait with as much interest as you to see if they did it. Obviously, it was a very, very bad mistake.'

Gerry Adams, President of Sinn Fein, broke his silence on the Monday afternoon, and he was more direct. He said: 'On behalf of the Republican people, I extend sympathy and condolences to the families and friends of those killed and injured yesterday in Enniskillen. I do not try to justify yesterday's bombing. I regret very much that it occurred.' Later in the week Sinn Fein councillors observed a minute's silence at the Finance Committee meeting of Derry City Council. The proposal came from Councillor Mitchell McLaughlin, who nearly eight years later was to attend Gordon's funeral in Enniskillen Methodist Church.

Some 30 hours after the explosion took place, the Provisional IRA admitted its responsibility for the bomb. It said that it 'deeply regretted' what had occurred, but claimed that the bomb had not been detonated 'by our radio signal'. The IRA suggested that the bomb could have been detonated by the security forces' scanners. This claim was dismissed angrily by the Northern Ireland Secretary of State, Tom King, as 'a totally pathetic, lame excuse to try to explain away one of the worst atrocities ever committed in Northern Ireland'. At the Enniskillen inquest later, a policeman said that the terrorists may have used information gathered from the Remembrance Day ceremony in 1986 to plan their attack a year later. The day after the bomb exploded, the Chief Constable of the RUC, Sir John Hermon, told a news conference that the building had not been searched by security forces, although they had searched the route of the parade. He said: 'The building and its location close to the area where the ceremony was held was less lethal to the security forces than anywhere else on the route they could have used. The decision not to search it, in those circumstances, was entirely proper.'

While such intense reaction was taking place publicly on a whole range of issues raised by the Enniskillen bomb, Gordon and Joan and their family and friends were grieving in private, and preparing for Marie's funeral. On the Monday morning, Gordon was taken back to the hospital for a check-up, and he then went to see his family doctor. One worry preying on his mind was whether or not he should go to see Marie's remains in the mortuary. Should he remember her in her vitality and youth, or lying in her coffin? His doctor strongly advised him to go to the mortuary, and Gordon was grateful for his advice. He said afterwards: 'My memories of Marie are predominantly of the good times, and my last sight of her was no more or less than saying goodbye to her mortal remains. The Marie I had known and loved was no longer there.'

Later that Monday afternoon, Marie's remains were brought to the Methodist church, where a short service was held prior to the funeral service on the Tuesday. Tom Magowan, the minister, had known the Wilsons ever since he had been an assistant minister in the church in 1956. He takes up the story:

I found Gordon a most generous-hearted man, both in his support of the work of the church, and in his dealings with his friends and those who came to him for help in his business, and in the public life of the community.

The Enniskillen bomb not only devastated the town but changed his life, and I faced the greatest challenge and crisis in my whole ministry as I ministered to the Wilson family and other families in the congregation who were bereaved and injured in the explosion. Out of the sorrow and heartbreak there emerged the spontaneous, riveting interview of Gordon that went around the world. That came straight from the heart, and was the expression of his Christian conviction and faith, nurtured from childhood in Christian teaching, and his firm belief in the infinite goodness and sovereignty of God, and the power of prayer to change things, as well as the Christian hope of life after death.

I marvelled at how he coped with the thousands of letters of sympathy that poured in from all over the world. I appealed to the media in the aftermath to give him and his family an opportunity to come to terms with their loss. It is said that behind every good man there is a good woman, and Joan Wilson epitomized this by her strong Christian faith and her support for Gordon when he returned home from the hectic round of interviews and television appearances or meetings. His daughter Julie Anne and his son Peter were also a source of encouragement to him. It was a privilege and a humbling experience for me as a Christian minister to care pastorally for the Wilson family at that time.

When it came to the funeral, Gordon was quite clear that he did not want to be any part of a media 'circus'. He insisted that no cameras would be permitted inside the church, and he wanted no political comment. 'I agreed wholeheartedly,' says Tom Magowan. 'We both realized that the tension was so high that a wrong word or unguarded comment would have precipitated open conflict. Gordon and Joan wanted it to be a service of thanksgiving, and the hymns and music were of their own choosing. In the event, it was a glorious celebration of the enabling power of Christ to triumph in the midst of tragedy. Indeed, I had many letters from people testifying to the inspiring nature of the service.'

Although the television cameras were not allowed in the church, the funeral was given widespread coverage. There was wisdom in the decision to refrain from making any political comment or any statements that might inflame, as tensions remained high. On the night of the explosion, the security forces foiled a massive bomb attack in Belfast's city centre, when they dismantled a bomb loaded with 1,200 pounds of explosives. Earlier, five Roman Catholic teenagers were attacked by gunfire on the city's Antrim Road, apparently in retaliation for the Enniskillen bombing. It also emerged that a 150-pound beer-keg bomb had been hidden in a hedgerow some 25 metres from the start of a Remembrance Day parade at Tullyhommon, on the Fermanagh border. It had a command wire leading across to the Irish Republic. A senior police officer said that he had no doubt that the two bombs were closely linked, and each was planned to cause maximum death and injury.

The town of Enniskillen virtually closed down for the funerals. Notices in shops and offices said simply, 'Closed – in deepest sympathy'. Marie Wilson's funeral took place at noon, around the same time as that of another victim, Edward Armstrong, in the Presbyterian church. In the afternoon, the funeral of Samuel Gault was held at the local Church of Ireland cathedral. Each was different, and undoubtedly each meant different things to all those who took part, but the town was united in a common mourning.

Joan recalls: 'The funeral service generated for me a great sense of peace. We were totally shattered, but the music, the readings and the prayers were very uplifting. I believe that God was bringing all of us through. Gordon had said, "Let's get through this with as much dignity as we can," and that's what we tried to do. I remember Tom's wonderful address, and on the way out I recall the Church of Ireland Bishop of Clogher, the Right Reverend Brian Hannon, touching Gordon's arm and saying to him, "You are doing well." That meant a lot to Gordon. Julie Anne was a tower of strength, even though she was breaking up inside. She was very, very upset, particularly after the funeral.'

Julie Anne says: 'There have been so many funerals in the family, including those of Marie, Peter and Dad, that I have to think hard sometimes to remember the different details of each. I remember being very emotional at Marie's funeral, and I would have cried very easily. Mum and Dad were very strong, and it was almost as if we were not allowed to cry. Mum's father had lost a leg in the First World War, and he was one of the old "stiff upper lip" generation. So I got through the funeral as best I could. At times I had to keep myself from screaming out loud, but I didn't want to make a complete fool of myself. We did not let our emotions show publicly in any way, but we were all absolutely churning up inside.'

The officiating clergy included Dr Hedley Plunkett, Marie's uncle, who read a passage of Scripture; Alan Hanna, who had baptized Marie as a baby in that very church; and the current minister, Tom Magowan, who in many ways had the most difficult task of all – that of finding the right words for such an occasion. His address was equal to the challenge, as he spoke with great sensitivity about the death of Marie and the unspeakable loss to the Wilson family. He also spoke about the great wave of love and compassion from the entire community for all the bereaved and injured.

He said: 'You tell me Marie Wilson is dead, and presently we will lay to rest her mortal remains with much love. I saw the spirit of Marie in the Casualty Department of the Erne Hospital. I saw the spirit of Marie in the wave of compassion and practical caring that crossed over the religious divide as a shattered community came close together in love and succour for the bereaved and injured. Though we sorrow today, we do not sorrow as a people without hope. The secret of the radiant, vital life of Marie came from her personal faith in Jesus Christ as her Saviour and Lord.'

As the funeral cortege made its way to the cemetery, it passed the Presbyterian church where the service for Edward Armstrong was taking place. Gordon said later: 'It was a forceful reminder that we were not the only ones suffering that day. We laid Marie to rest in the Enniskillen graveyard. The final prayers were said, and then the blessing, and we left Marie's remains in that freshly filled grave. It was just

Gordon as a young man in 1950

Gordon and Joan on their
wedding day in 1955

Gordon with his father, George, and son, Peter

Marie

Gordon at home, with Marie's photograph

Marie at home

Gordon meets the Prince and Princess of Wales at Enniskillen, shortly after the 1987 bombing

Gordon with the World Methodist Peace Award. From left to right: Dr Joe Hale, General Secretary of the World Methodist Council, Gordon, Bishop Lawi Imathiu, Chairman of the World Methodist Council, and Rev T S Whittington, President of the Methodist Church in Ireland

Gordon at the launch of the Spirit of Enniskillen bursaries, with Dr Brian Mawhinney, then Education Minister in Northern Ireland (centre), and Gerry Burns, then Clerk and Chief Executive of Fermanagh District Council (right)

over two days since she had stood by my side, young and lovely and alive. And now she was gone. We went back home to try to face whatever the future would hold for all of us.'

The day after Marie was buried, the Wilson family began the task of trying to pick up the pieces of their shattered lives. There were people to see, details to be attended to, and a hundred and one small demands which might seem mundane but which also bring a kind of practical and vital continuity. It is a truism that 'life must go on', but that, literally, is what happens after a bereavement. Some time later Gordon reflected on the inner turmoil amidst the daily round of ordinary duties. It dawned only slowly and painfully that Marie had gone. He said: 'There was no blinding flash, or a point of time when the truth sank in. It was like someone lowering a blind inch by inch, rather than shutting the light out suddenly. Some days are better than others, but then there are times when it is totally bleak, and we feel as if we are back to square one.'

Even the most ordinary tasks were difficult. Gordon was so incapacitated that Joan had to wash his hair, and while doing so she realized yet again the physical trauma he had suffered – the discolouration, the bruises, and even the fact that she still had to wash away traces of the dust and debris from the bomb which had matted his hair.

However, there was little time for domestic respite. Two days after the funeral, a memorial service for the victims was held in the local Roman Catholic church, and after thinking it over and taking counsel with a few close friends, Gordon decided to attend, 'to show personal solidarity with and compassion for all those who had lost loved ones, from whatever background they were'. To observers from outside Northern Ireland, such a service would have seemed a natural occurrence in a predominantly Christian community. But in Irish terms it was deeply symbolic. The bomb blast at the Enniskillen Cenotaph was widely interpreted as an attack on the Protestant community by those who largely had their roots in a broadly Roman Catholic background. That is not to say that Roman Catholics approved of the violence or of the IRA. On the contrary, Roman Catholic clergy and laity were ever at pains to condemn such violence. Indeed, on the night after the

Enniskillen bombing the Roman Catholic Bishops had issued a firm and unequivocal statement on the question of support for violence. It said: 'There is no room for ambivalence. In face of the present campaigns of Republican violence, the choice for all Catholics is clear. It is a choice between good and evil. It is sinful to join organizations committed to violence or to remain in them. It is sinful to support such organizations or to call on others to support them.' The condemnation could not have been clearer.

The service in St Michael's Roman Catholic Church sent a strong signal to the wider community. In the words of the *Belfast Telegraph*, it 'gave real signs of hope that the Protestant and Roman Catholic communities devastated by the Remembrance Sunday massacre could strive to face the future together'. Though Gordon Wilson knew that he and other Protestants might be criticized for attending such a service and that they might be accused of 'selling out' their own denominations, he decided to go anyway – as did a local Church of Ireland rector, the Reverend John McCarthy, pupils from the mainly Protestant Portora Royal School, and other Protestants from the Enniskillen area.

Gordon was accompanied by Derrick Haskins, the Assistant Minister of Gordon's church. When they went into St Michael's Church they were led to seats near the front (Gordon had asked for seats at the back). As they walked up the aisle, the 1,500-strong congregation burst into spontaneous applause. Gordon said: 'I was totally flabbergasted. I couldn't believe my eyes or ears!' He found the service itself very moving. 'I had a feeling that I had never experienced in quite the same way before, nor have I since. I felt that I was in the very presence of God.'

He reflected later: 'Some people asked me afterwards why I had gone to the Catholic service. There had not been much time to think about motives or reasons for going, but something inside told me that the Catholic people of Enniskillen were making an important gesture to all the families of the eleven who had died. They were willing to pray for us, to extend the hands of friendship and love. They were not merely saying, "We are sorry for your trouble." They were saying in an even deeper sense, "We are truly *sorry*." It is important to make the point that Derek Haskins and I were not the only Protestants in the church that night. The Catholics were offering friendship, and that was most important. The eleven who had died were all Protestant, and I felt that the Protestant people in Enniskillen were willing to receive any gesture of friendship, little or large, that was offered.' Inevitably, Gordon was criticized. 'The attitude of hostility from a minority of Protestants made me very sad. I felt that I was right to go. It was a natural response, a very human gesture, seeking solace and healing.'

The service was attended by Cardinal Tomas O'Fiaich and the local Catholic Bishop, the Most Reverend Dr Joseph Duffy. Afterwards Gordon had a private meeting with the Cardinal, who also made brave headlines that week when he apologized on behalf of his co-religionists for the wrongs done in their name. Already it looked as if remarkable things were happening in the wake of the Enniskillen explosion.

A week later, attention focused on the Irish Republic, where a one-minute silence was held nationwide, and a service took place at St Patrick's Church of Ireland Cathedral in Dublin, where public and community leaders from all over Ireland had come to pay their respects to the Enniskillen dead and injured. The preacher was the Right Reverend Brian Hannon, the Church of Ireland Bishop of Clogher, who was quickly on the scene in Enniskillen on the day of the explosion. In a forceful and moving sermon which drew spontaneous applause from all those present (this reduced him to tears), the Bishop captured in his words the magnitude of the evil at Enniskillen, and also asked the hard questions that had to be faced if there was to be a better way forward. He asked if the Enniskillen bombing would be any different from

> any of our other ghastly nine-day wonders? I believe it is. After twenty-four hours I said publicly that this could be the catalyst, the cross-roads, the turning-point in the history of our troubles. There are signs of such change. The change of mind can be seen most obviously in a growing belief that violence leads only to pain, chaos, division and despair. The change of heart is experienced in growing revulsion at the inhuman and deepening obscenities of violence, realizing that we are being dragged into a quicksand of amoral depravity. And the change of will is being felt

in the growing determination of individuals, churches and of our states that violence must not be allowed to win. Mind, heart and will; all the ingredients of conversion, of a turning-point and a change in direction.

The Bishop did not mince his words. He asked the assembled congregation, and those people listening to the televised service, some very pointed questions:

Do you believe that the others who live in this island, no matter what their origin, have a right to stay here and to share responsibility for the state in which they live? Do you believe that members of other Christian denominations can be just as genuine and true followers of Jesus Christ as you are? In other words, since I am a member of the 'Church of Ireland', should I assume that we are the Church of Ireland, and it is simply a pity that everyone else doesn't know any better? Or if you are a Roman Catholic, do you assume that you are the Catholic Church and that therefore everyone else is obviously non-Catholic? Or if you simply say 'Ah, but I'm a Christian', do you assume that everyone else who hasn't qualified your way is not?

Such an eloquent plea for a better, more tolerant and more pluralistic society was one of the many fruits of a widening awareness of community and individual interdependence and joint responsibility in the aftermath of that remarkable week of the Enniskillen bombing, but there was still much to be done. The letters page in the *Belfast Telegraph* on the Friday before the Bishop's challenging words in Dublin reinforced the reality that the Enniskillen bombing brought out the best and the worst in society. The headline read 'All one in our suffering', but some of the letter-writers expressed the great degree of division and bitterness which was still rooted in the community. Gordon Wilson's words, and the Enniskillen carnage, had not changed the world, but they had begun to raise the practical question of how violence could be eliminated from the Irish equation for ever.

7

In the Wilderness

During the days and weeks after the funeral, Gordon and Joan received literally thousands of letters of sympathy from all over the United Kingdom, the Irish Republic and further afield. There were so many that the Post Office had to make special deliveries to the Wilson home at Cooper Crescent. Messages and letters came from a very wide range of people, including the Queen, the Duke of Edinburgh, Prime Minister Margaret Thatcher, and many others. Often they were signed in utter simplicity as, for example, 'Jim from Bristol'. There were so many that a friend who was in charge of the Commerce Department in Fermanagh College of Further Education asked his secretarial students to sort incoming mail and to type the names and addresses for the replies. Gordon said: 'Some were lyrically beautiful. We found them helpful, but even more helpful on a second reading, because it was impossible to take in immediately the significance of what they were saying and the way they said it. I made a point of reading every letter. People were so kind. Partly as a result of that experience, I now write letters to people who have been and are suffering, and, hopefully, I now write with better understanding. Oddly, I find it more difficult to express my sympathy, because I know that I can't write nearly as well as some of the people who wrote to us.'

There was, however, a handful of hostile and abusive letters. Tom Magowan recalls: 'There were maybe two dozen of this kind of letter which Gordon showed to me. He was a bit taken aback that people could write that sort of letter, but I advised him not to worry. I said that these were anonymous letters and did not signify, though we decided not to show them to Joan.'

The Wilsons also received a great many flowers, in bouquets, in pots and in baskets. Many donors asked that the flowers be placed on Marie's grave, and even three years later Gordon and Joan were still receiving cheques to buy flowers in Marie's memory. They used to find fresh flowers laid regularly on her grave, and they never knew who had placed them there. Joan says: 'This is still happening and I am still moved and grateful. I can hardly believe it.'

Gordon and Joan and their family also met a number of VIPs during these days, including the Prince and Princess of Wales. Joan was particularly impressed by Prince Charles, who had spoken to her with great sympathy. Gordon was equally impressed, and also noted privately that 'Princess Diana is even prettier than she looks from her photographs!' (Perhaps this was an early hint of the old Gordon re-emerging – he always noticed an attractive woman!) The general conclusion was that the Royal couple coped well on what must have been for them a difficult visit, and their very presence in Enniskillen lifted people's spirits.

Some weeks later, Gordon himself was humbled and honoured to be mentioned by name in the Queen's 1987 Christmas broadcast. He had wind of it when a tabloid reporter, obviously breaking a Royal embargo, phoned Gordon in advance of the broadcast to ask if he had any comment. Wisely, he said nothing, but he was not surprised when Her Majesty's Lieutenant for County Fermanagh called on Christmas Eve to tell him officially about the next day's broadcast. The Queen spoke of the way in which Gordon Wilson had impressed the whole world by the depth of his forgiveness. She went on: 'His strength, and that of his wife, and the courage of their daughter, came from their Christian conviction. All of us will echo their prayer that out of the personal tragedies of Enniskillen may come a reconciliation between the communities.' Gordon was moved by the Queen's words, but he was equally struck when, a few days later, a tea-lady at the Royal Victoria Hospital came up to him unannounced and said, 'God bless you and thank you, and I'm sorry for your trouble.' He commented: 'Sincerely expressed sympathy has no boundaries and no barriers, whether it's from the Queen herself, or a tea-lady in the Royal Victoria Hospital.'

It was unusual for an individual to be named in the Queen's Christmas broadcast, but it illustrated the fact that Gordon Wilson's fame was spreading far and wide, and this made him uneasy. He found it difficult to come to terms with living in the public spotlight. Sometimes it amused him, as when he was voted 'Man of the Year' in a BBC Radio Four poll – ahead of Mr Gorbachev and Prince Charles! As Gordon said: 'It was all a long way from the draper's shop in Enniskillen!' A number of awards were to come his way, but he never felt totally at ease accepting them, because he was always conscious that many others from Enniskillen, and elsewhere, had also suffered grievous loss. He never tired of saying that he was representing only Marie Wilson and her family.

Some of the presentations were particularly poignant, such as that in the Dorchester Hotel in London, where he accepted a posthumous award for Marie, who was remembered as a 'Woman of Courage' in the 1987 Women of Achievement Awards. There were several other awards, including the title 'Man of the Year' from the Royal Association for Disability and Rehabilitation, and a 1988 'People of the Year' Award in Ireland. Later on, he received the prestigious 'World Methodist Peace Award', which pleased him greatly. Gordon accepted these and other awards graciously and thoughtfully. He said later: 'I did my best to meet people where they were, with their thoughts and sympathy and awards expressed in their own way, knowing that it was all part of a greater whole which in some way, some day, would contribute to a greater peace in our own land.'

In public, Gordon put on a brave face. But privately he had faced an immense and agonizing personal struggle in the weeks and months following the explosion. Only his family and close friends were aware of the depth of the darkness which he had to come through. He was in constant demand for media interviews, and while these gave him a purpose and a sense of achievement, they also drained him. Joan says: 'The media kept coming, from France, America, Switzerland, from all over the world, and Gordon just couldn't refuse them. I hated all of that, but it was a therapy to him. If it had been me, I would have turned them away, but I felt sorry for them as people. They had a job to do, and when Gordon invited them in, the least I could do was give them a cup of tea and something to eat. Anyway, there was no need for me to appear in the media, because Gordon did it so well.'

The media also absorbed Gordon in a personal way. Julie Anne recalls: 'In the weeks after the funeral, he used to play and replay the video tapes of the Enniskillen bomb and its aftermath. Maybe it was a kind of therapy in its own way, but it also seemed like a kind of depression. It was almost a morbid interest in what had taken place. He was oblivious to this, and it got so bad that we put our foot down and took the tapes away.' The pressure of the interviews, the tapes, the thousands of letters waiting for a reply, and his own frail physical and emotional condition took a cumulative toll. Seven weeks after the bomb, he completely lost his memory, and was admitted to hospital.

Joan recalls the moment she knew something was terribly wrong. 'He began to talk complete nonsense. He said to me, "When is Marie coming home?" Then he asked, "Why do I have this awful pain in my shoulder?" I was on the phone to our family doctor immediately, because I thought it might be the reoccurrence of a mild stroke he had had several years previously. When the doctor arrived, Gordon turned to me and asked, "Who is this stranger in our house?" He had flipped completely. Without delay, we took him to the Erne Hospital for observation. It was really worrying.'

Julie Anne takes up the story: 'I feared that Dad was losing his marbles, that he was really starting to crumble. It was frightening. Everything was so bleak for us. I remember him vividly in hospital. He could not recall anything about the bomb, or about Marie, or why he was in pain. It was hard for us to deal with this. He was like that for maybe 16 to 24 hours, and the next morning he had recovered. I went into the ward, and he was sitting up and behaving just like normal. I threw my arms around him and said, "Dad, you're back with us again! Thank God!"'

As a precaution he was taken to the Royal Victoria Hospital for a brain-scan, and was given the all-clear. But the visit to the Royal, where Marie had been a nurse just a few weeks previously, was a stern test for Joan. She says: 'It had so many memories of Marie. I got myself into an awful state, thinking of what it would be like to go up there and to see all these other young girls walking about in nurses' uniforms. Peter drove us to Belfast, and I remember sitting in the car and trying to rationalize, trying to tell myself, "Don't be frightened. You're going to a place of healing. All these young nurses and the doctors and other people are doing all they can to make people better." That kind of thinking helped me. Once we were in the hospital, I met an orderly who had known Marie. He said, "Many a day she helped me to wheel patients to the theatre, and many a cheery greeting and quip we had. She was a great girl." That also helped me enormously. I should have known that it would be all right. I remembered also the reports of a Thanksgiving Service which was held at the Royal just after Marie died. We were too exhausted to go personally, but I know that the Reverend Sydney Callaghan gave a wonderful address. He talked about "the burden that the mother-heart bore too, in that Joan Wilson shared those closing hours with Marie. And we must not overlook that agony and anguish that any mother will understand in a way that no father can fully comprehend." I was grateful for those kind and sensitive words.'

The doctors concluded that the strain and pressure of the previous weeks had led to the loss of memory, but Gordon recovered quickly, and without any further relapse. A family holiday to the Caribbean, which they had had to postpone due to Gordon's illness, took place in February 1988. It was a break which they all needed very badly. Julie Anne reflects: 'It was as if three different people went on holiday. We all needed our own space. Personally, it did me good to get away from Enniskillen and to realize that there was a big world outside, and that this world was not shrouded in darkness. I met a lovely girl and we became friends. I was able to talk to her, and she helped me tremendously. We still stay in touch. I remember particularly that she enjoyed meeting Dad. She called him "Gordon", and Dad didn't seem to mind, though he was one of the "old school" and really didn't like younger people calling him by his Christian name. If you were younger than he was, you gave him his proper title. Even my husband John used to call him "Mr Wilson", almost up to the day he died!'

Julie Anne also discovered a side to her father which he tried to keep hidden from the family, but which showed the depths of his private grief. 'During the day, Dad seemed fine, and in company he was the life and soul of the party. But we knew privately that he could not sleep very well, and that he used to get up early in the morning and pace around the deck of the cruise ship. One of the passengers told me later that one morning he was also up and about early, and he observed Dad grieving alone by the ship's rail and crying out to sea. But it was never mentioned by any of us.'

Joan remembers the cruise as a breathing-space and as therapy: 'It was good for all of us, just to get away from it all and to be our own people. I met a lady who had lost her husband in an air crash, and she was most understanding. I remember walking with her on the beach at St Thomas, where she shared her experience of bereavement with me. She said, "The grief is like the waves rolling on to this beach. Sometimes the grief will come over you in waves, and they will threaten to overwhelm you. Then they will recede. They will come again at longer intervals, but eventually, with time, they will begin to ease, and you will find yourself better able to cope." That was sound advice, and she gave me great help.'

Back in Enniskillen, Gordon and Joan grieved differently – sometimes together, and more often privately. She says: 'He was able to cry long before I was. He used to go into a room and I could hear this terrible sobbing behind closed doors, and I did not intrude. It was an intensely private thing. He never talked about it, and I never let him know that I heard it happening. It helped him, and that was what he needed. Gordon cried alone, and at night. I did my crying outdoors. My crying was dreadful, but it made me feel better. The first time was the worst, but after that I was not afraid to let myself go.'

Her father had always urged her to keep a stiff upper lip. People of his generation did not cry; it was seen as a form of weakness. 'One day, however, I was walking along the lovely paths at Castle Coole, and I saw the snowdrops pushing up through the ground in the middle of a long winter, with their promise of spring. I could not help thinking about our own long winter of Marie's death, and I just cried and cried, in the privacy of nature. I could hardly stop the flood-gates. But I knew that this was a necessary part of my healing. I would now say to anyone in the midst of bereavement, "Don't be afraid to cry. Let yourself go. It's all part of your healing."'

Gordon and Joan went to the graveyard together, but on many occasions, each of them visited Marie's grave alone. Joan says, 'Sometimes I used to go there straight from school or from shopping. I used to stand there and just think of her. Marie's twenty-first birthday was dreadful – the 29th of April 1988. I took flowers to her grave and I spoke out loud, as if she had been there. I said, "I'm sorry, my darling, that I can't bring you a special present for your birthday. All I can bring you is flowers for your grave." I cried and cried. Gordon was quiet. He simply said, "Marie's gone. We'll just have to do the best we can."

'There were other times when we grieved together, very often on long car journeys. We talked about Marie, and we used to ask ourselves, "Why did it happen? Why did it happen to us?" But we would also ask ourselves, "Why not?" We were not the only ones grieving. There were ten other families in Enniskillen, and families all over the British Isles and further afield who were grieving because of the suffering of the Troubles. Gordon would also say to me, from time to time, "I've been through a bomb." It was almost as if he could hardly take in the fact that he had lost Marie and he had been in the explosion as well. He was also very conscious of the others who had been killed and injured. He often wondered why people standing only a few feet from him had died, and he had been spared. It was all part of his sense of mission at being left to tell the story of Marie and of the suffering.'

The relatives of the Enniskillen victims met a number of times. Joan remembers: 'This was early on, and I believe that these meetings helped us. But as time went on and we gained strength, there seemed less of a need to meet. I am still very aware of what is happening to the others, and I keep up an interest. I noticed recently that a grandchild of Willie and Nessie Mullan had done very well at school and was going on to university. His grandparents would have been very proud of him. I remember, too, a lovely visit on the Christmas Eve after Marie died, when Aileen Quinton came to our doorstep. Her mother, Georgina Quinton, who had been a nurse, had also died in the Enniskillen bomb. Aileen gave me a table-cloth which she had started to crochet for her mother before the bomb. She said to me, "The older nurse has gone. I would like to present this to the mother of the younger nurse." It was a beautiful gesture, and it touched me deeply.'

After the bomb, Gordon lost interest in his business. Joan says: 'He now saw life in a totally different perspective. Things which had been important to him previously did not seem to matter any more. Anyhow, he was just not fit for it. Luckily, he had no money worries, and he just wanted to let it go at the best price possible. Peter had taken on the major brunt of running the business, and this was not easy for him. He had his own challenges to face. Eventually, the business was sold, and Peter went out on his own. It seemed the best solution in the circumstances, because there was just no way that Gordon could continue.'

He found some solace in the ordinary things of life. He resumed his regular morning-coffee sessions with his friends in Enniskillen, and his golf-partners coaxed him back on to the course. Joe Prenter, who himself had undergone heart surgery, recalls going with Gordon to the golf course merely to look. They discovered that Gordon had a five-iron and some golf-balls in his car. They both tried their swing, and to their surprise and delight, they could still hit a ball – just! Joe says: 'That was the beginning of our come-back!' At first Gordon could hardly hold the club, but he persevered, and golf at his beloved Murvagh course again became a part of his life.

However, there were some things which he could not change. Joan recalls: 'After the bomb, he could not stand any loud noises. If I dropped even a knife on the floor, his nerves would jangle. He could not even bear a child's toy screeching across the floor. He always said that the bomb had been a dull thud, rather than a loud blast, but he could not bear anything loud. He became very, very sensitive to noise. I took account of that and tried to guard against dropping things or making a loud noise.'

Their shared trauma brought them closer. Joan says: 'I felt that I had to take even more care of him, because after the bomb he tired very easily. We were also conscious of cherishing our time together and of living each day more fully. It made us more aware of the sufferings of other people, when we heard about other tragedies on the news, or closer to home. We really felt for people. When you have experienced a deep trauma yourself, you have something special to give to others who are caught up in suffering. It made us realize how important it is to try to share the burden. We received tremendous help from people's letters and especially from their prayers. Gordon used to say that we were surrounded by such a wall of prayer that you could almost touch it.'

Gordon and Joan also derived great comfort from Marie's former flat-mates, Katherine, Fiona and Claire, who all trained as nurses at the Royal Victoria Hospital. Gordon once reflected: 'They have been extremely good to us. They have come together to see us, and on their own. They have been extremely faithful in putting anniversary notices in the paper and in placing flowers on Marie's grave. We have been keeping in touch with them from our end, and we have been to the weddings of all of the girls. At a time like that you think long of Marie and of what might have been, but you put those kinds of thoughts out of your mind and you think only of the girls and of their happiness. We hope dearly that they will stay in touch and that they will drop in to see us. We need their support more than they need ours, and that's why we always love to see them. They bring a breath of fresh air into our lives, just the way Marie did when she came breezing in for a weekend at home.'

There was great inherent strength in the Wilson family. Though Gordon and Joan were in the public eye, they had unstinting support from Julie Anne, Peter and his wife Ingrid behind the scenes. They all needed their own space, but they were always ready to help with the many practical details of life, and also to share one another's grief. Gordon recalled talking to Peter one evening about the pressures of life, and the tragedy of Marie's death, and they both ended in tears. As well as the tears, there was a bedrock of solid Ulster stoicism and practicality. Julie Anne says: 'I desperately needed space, and my own time to come to terms with what had happened. But I also knew what the others were going through, and I understood Dad's need to talk it out, even through the media. I felt that it was good for him, in a strange way, though we always tried to ensure that he would not exhaust himself.'

The Wilsons' neighbours and close friends were constantly supportive, from the time of the explosion and Marie's death, when they quickly organized refreshments for those who called to pay their respects. And this support continued for weeks and months afterwards. There was support, too, from total strangers, including a family who travelled from Dublin to the Methodist church in Enniskillen on the Sunday after the explosion to convey the sympathies of their local prayer-group. All of this, plus an endless stream of letters, sympathy cards and flowers provided a wide network of support which helped Gordon and Joan and the family enormously.

Looking back on those early weeks, Gordon said: 'To any families who are suffering bereavement, I would say unhesitatingly, "Please accept the offers of help from your friends and neighbours. It can't be easy for them either, but they will give you the support which you will need and appreciate." The long experience has taught me that there's no purpose in being a recluse, in sitting in a corner and crying your eyes out. You have to put on a brave face and step out into the world. In nine cases out of ten, people will rally magnificently and help you. I now know what it is like to be bereaved and to try to share that experience with others, and hopefully to bring a dimension which will be helpful and relevant. The poet John Donne wrote, "No man is an island", and we found out how true that was.'

It took Gordon a long time to try to come to terms with Marie's death, and in one sense he never completely succeeded in doing so. But his strength increased little by little, as did Joan's. He had no idea what lay ahead of him, in terms of his mission in the public eye, but he was aware of the need 'to put on a brave face and to step out into the world'. And as he turned to face that world, there were glimmers of light amid the gloom.

8

Opening Out

Though he was always naturally outgoing, Gordon was also a very private person. He once remarked, with a typically earthy wit, that one of the best things about selling the shop and retiring from the drapery business was that he no longer felt obliged to greet every customer in the street – though he would have had a cheery word for most of them anyway! His natural attitude after the bomb was a combination of surprise and reticence – surprise that his words had caused such an instant reaction and that the media kept coming back, and also a reticence to open old wounds.

There was also a third dimension, to add to the complexity. While he did not wish to place himself once again in the spotlight, he wrestled privately with a sense of mission. He believed deeply that God had spared him in the explosion to try to share with other people the horrific reality of violence and also to convey to the world the necessity of forgiveness and reconciliation, and the power of love, which had been symbolized in Marie's last words as she lay under the rubble. Ostensibly he wanted to tell Marie's story, but he also wanted to impress on people the utter futility of violence. He was not a man to speak with the detachment of an academic observer, but as one who had been in a bomb-blast and had lived to tell the tale, whereas his daughter and ten other people had not.

Gordon had been struggling with these conflicting motives for nearly a year when, out of the blue, he was asked to write a book about his experiences. The call came from Christine Smith, of the London publishers HarperCollins. She says: 'I remember the moment when I heard Gordon's first broadcast. It was so powerful that I was absolutely rooted to the spot. This was an exceptional man speaking from the depths of an enormous tragedy, yet with compassion and understanding. It was utterly compelling. It stayed in my mind, and about a year later I wrote to Gordon, but I was fearful of intruding on a grief that was too immense for words.'

No reply came, but suddenly, weeks later, there was a phone-call from Gordon to acknowledge Christine's letter, and to let her know that he did not want to write a book. He had written a three-page reply which he had not posted, and he asked if he could read it out to her on the phone. As he went through the reasons why he was not keen to write a book, ranging from his lack of experience of writing, to his tiredness and his unwillingness to re-open old wounds, Christine began to get the impression that he was not convinced by what he was saying. 'I realized that he was not in fact saying "No", but was rather asking me to persuade him to say "Yes".' Christine asked if they could meet the next time she was over in Northern Ireland, which happened to be some four months later.

'I travelled to Enniskillen and met him in the shop. His office was perched like a gallery on the far wall, allowing him to gaze over the entire activity of the shop. I had expected to meet a rather frail, elderly man, but when I saw Gordon I was pleasantly shocked. He was stat-uesque, with a great sense of style and presence, and later I could see how he carried off the position of Senator so well. He *looked* like a Senator!

'We began to talk about the possibility of a book, but he was emphatic that he did not want to rake up the past – it was just too painful. He was also worried that his motives might be questioned and that some people would accuse him of capitalizing on Marie's death. Already he had received several wounding comments, including one particularly savage phone-call from a woman who accused him of "dancing on Marie's grave".'

There was no apparent progress on the book idea, but Christine sensed that a seed had been planted. About six months later he phoned Christine to tell her that he was coming to London. 'I knew then that he was interested. We met again, and he said that he would give it a try. I believe that he had wanted to say "Yes" much earlier, but he didn't know how to begin and was nervous about being misunderstood. But his sense of mission prevailed. He bought a tape recorder and tried talking into it, but that didn't work. He had an important story to tell and a unique perspective on peace and reconciliation – not as a politician, but as someone whom "ordinary" people listened to, who could inspire the man and the woman in the street, and who, above all, had a right to be heard. But it was clear that he was going to need a writer to work with him.'

Christine rang me at my desk in Belfast before she first approached Gordon, and I told her that I thought he was too private a man to venture into print. Like everyone else, I was overwhelmed by Gordon's first broadcast and could scarcely believe what I was hearing, in a Province which had become so used to the most awful suffering. During the week of the Enniskillen funerals, I was visiting the war graves at the Somme in Northern France, and the horror of all violence, including that of Enniskillen, seemed so utterly wasteful and universal. Several weeks later the news of Gordon's loss of memory was reported by the media, and I was not in the least surprised, given the suffering he had gone through. His tragedy, like that of so many others, was part of the dull ache which we all had felt for so long in Ulster, without seeming to be able to do much about it. And in the steady blood-drip of violence, the sharp pain of Enniskillen receded into the general ache of the community-wide despair. But the conversation about a book remained open-ended.

Quite some time later Christine rang me again and said that Gordon had agreed to try to produce a book. I was surprised and delighted by the invitation to work with Gordon, but I didn't know what to expect from this person with the extraordinary reputation. We met one Sunday afternoon at a hotel mid-way between Belfast and Enniskillen. From the start I trusted and liked this tall, angular man with the direct gaze and the firm handshake. He had a brisk, no-nonsense attitude, and his motives struck me as impeccable. He wanted to produce a book which would tell Marie's story simply but without sentimentality. He wished to share his experience of dealing with grief, in an effort to help others, and he was honest enough to admit that this in itself might help his own healing. And he did not wish to open old wounds, including those of the others who had suffered as a result of the Enniskillen bomb. Despite his inner sense of mission, he looked and sounded frail, and I wondered if he could sustain the energy for such a project.

Nevertheless, we agreed on a plan of action. He would ponder on an initial set of broad questions from me, and we would work our way through the Marie story from beginning to end. This meant travelling to his home in Enniskillen at regular intervals and spending weekends locked together in detailed conversations which were tape-recorded. During these meetings he bared his soul and told me some things which he had previously kept hidden within the family circle. Those visits, apart from the professional progress we made, remain a precious personal memory to me, because I was accepted as one of the family and I grew to admire Gordon's integrity and courage and to enjoy his sense of humour and conviviality. I also came to value Joan's enormous kindness, and also her deep resources of inner strength and spirituality, and the fact that she deliberately *chose* to take a back seat in order to help Gordon – a point which was not generally recognized by the public.

As the book slowly took shape over the next year or so, Gordon continued to worry about opening old wounds and about providing an opportunity for people to criticize him. Curiously, he also worried about his ability to acquit himself properly on the media when the book was published – a point which concerned me not at all, because Gordon was a natural performer. However, I occasionally wondered if he would survive to see the book published, because when his guard dropped, he did seem frail. He smoked too much, and it seemed almost a miracle that his battered body was able to sustain him. Gradually, however, I noticed an improvement. The book really began to enthuse him, because it encapsulated all that he cared about – namely, Marie's story and all that it represented. Next to Joan and the family, this was his whole life.

The writing and the publication of the book took place with hardly a hitch. Gordon's fears proved groundless, while the project itself gave him the therapy he so badly needed. However, there were two significant and symbolic episodes which stay in my mind. One of these concerned telling the story of the moment of Marie's death. I had not realized that

Gordon had not been at Marie's bedside with the rest of the family. It was Joan who told me about Marie's last moments, in words so powerful, simple and eloquent that they would have brought tears from a stone. Unfortunately Gordon could not see the point of including Joan's words in what was *his* account of Marie's life and death. I tried to put Joan's words in the third person, but their dramatic impact was lost. Deadlock loomed, but one day after lunch I said to Gordon privately, 'Listen to this. I'm going to read out Joan's words, and they should go into the book exactly as I read them.' He listened in absolute silence while I read him the words which even then, though I had read them dozens of times, moved me to fresh tears. There was a pause, and then he said slowly, 'You're right. They should go in.' That was all he said, and the subject was never mentioned again. I was surprised, and a bit taken aback, that he had such difficulty in accepting that Joan's voice should be included in this way. I was never sure whether Gordon, with his precise, matter-of-fact mind, ever really understood why a voice other than his own should appear in a book which was ostensibly written by him – or whether he was relegating Joan to the background in what he was beginning to see as *his* story.

Joan's powers of description were equal to his and sometimes better, and I wondered whether Gordon was afraid of being upstaged. It was a topic I chose not to pursue, and I gave him the benefit of the doubt. I knew that he was a man of his generation who believed that women should remain in the background, but I was also aware that he was most protective of Joan, and he knew how much he depended upon her. In the book, he went out of his way to underline his debt to her. He wrote, 'There are no words in my vocabulary to express what I owe to Joan. She is my wife, partner, friend, the one "who puts up with me", and also the mother of my children. You can't get any closer than that.' He also felt hurt if she was not always accorded the same honour as he was, such as the time when he was invited to lunch at Buckingham Palace but she was not. Nevertheless, I realized that behind Gordon's genial surface there was a tough, sometimes cutting, edge.

The other tussle we had was over the word 'forgiveness'. Though the media and the world at large adopted the short-hand description of

Gordon Wilson as the man who had 'forgiven' the IRA, his words on the night when Marie died had patently excluded the term 'forgiveness'. He had said, 'I bear no ill-will', which is not quite the same thing. We talked about this at great length, and painfully teased out his philosophy on this complex issue. He believed that the people who were responsible for the eleven deaths in Enniskillen would have to face the judgement of God, which 'is way beyond the forgiveness of Gordon Wilson'. Evil on that scale, he felt, was beyond human forgiveness and was of such a proportion that only the judgement of God himself could deal with it. However, in human terms he tried his very hardest to be forgiving, and he continued to pray for the bombers every night. After much debate and heart-searching, he concluded: 'Better men than me have wrestled with the whole concept of forgiveness and have failed. I believe that I do my very best in human terms to show forgiveness, but the last word rests with God, and those who seek his forgiveness will need to repent. At that level, such a judgement is way beyond me. All I can do is to continue not to think evil or malicious thoughts about these people and to go on bearing them no ill-will. I wasn't angry at the time, and I'm not angry now.'

And yet probably because of the media portrayal, Gordon became known as the man who had 'forgiven' his daughter's killers. Some people found it difficult to understand how Gordon could react in this way. Many felt that he had no 'right' to forgive those who had killed his daughter and ten other innocent people. They felt he was too quick to forgive, especially in a community where the Old Testament law of 'an eye for an eye' was uppermost in many people's minds. They failed to understand how Gordon himself wrestled with the whole concept of forgiveness, and that he felt that the last word rested with God.

Father Brian D'Arcy recognizes that when people think of Gordon Wilson, the word that springs to mind is 'forgiveness', and that a forgiveness which is real must transfer itself from the head to the heart and also to the gut. Too often our attitude is 'I can forgive you in my head, but my heart doesn't, and my gut will never forgive you.' He feels that Gordon Wilson forgave from head, heart and gut. 'He did not forgive easily, because it cost him. You had only to look at his pressured brow to know how much it was costing him, and it was not a forgiveness that was based on forgetting. It was a forgiveness that he had to re-enact every day when he got up...It was not a one-off thing.'

The book was launched in the autumn of 1990, to immediate success. Gordon was invited to appear on the vastly popular *Late, Late Show* on RTE television in Dublin. He was nervous about this, but after a slightly hesitant start, he spoke impressively. Joan, sitting in the front row of the audience in the cavernous studio, was even more apprehensive – particularly when the host, Gay Byrne, stepped across to her during the show and asked her a question. He went right to the heart of the matter and said, 'Tell us, Joan, how Marie died.' Joan, caught unaware, struggled to find words to convey her thoughts and emotions, while Gay Byrne, a seasoned professional, chose to stay silent at a time when a less-experienced broadcaster might have panicked and tried to put words into her mouth. Eventually Joan found her composure and she again described eloquently, simply and movingly how she watched Marie die. It was dramatic and arresting because it transcended the usual talk of a chat show. Her words described life and death in authentic, stark terms, and they came from the heart. There was total silence in that huge studio while the large audience listened intently, and afterwards the switchboard was jammed with calls of sympathy. Joan, like Gordon, remained unaware of her capacity to move and to inspire, and to this day she is still unaware of the power of her insight and her gift for description.

The RTE broadcast was followed the next day by a book-signing session in Enniskillen, the first of many for Gordon throughout the British Isles. The book seemed to give him new strength and a new zest for living and for taking Marie's story to others. He had, literally in his hand, his mission-statement, his reason for taking on speaking engagements everywhere, and his point of contact for the very many people who wanted to share his mission with him. It was symbolic and significant that the only thing he carried with him to meet the IRA was a copy of *Marie*, which he held in his hand to give him strength and support. For me, it was – and still is – one of the most important books which it has been my privilege to write.

Joan looks back on this period as an important part of Gordon's healing. She believed that it provided great therapy for him, and gave him a sense of challenge and of adventure. 'It really was very precious to all of us, and not Gordon alone. He always felt that it was a lovely story, which was told with great dignity and sensitivity, and beautifully presented. It had an impact which he never dreamed possible. Wherever he went, the book went with him – all over Northern Ireland, to the Irish Republic, to Wales, Scotland and England, America, South Africa, Caribbean cruises, everywhere. It helped so many people who were in the midst of their suffering and bereavement.

'Gordon took part in book-signings everywhere, because he loved meeting people, talking to them, hearing their point of view. He once went to a signing in Lisburn, and the shop had to be cleared due to a bomb-scare. Unfortunately, he could not stay until it was over, because he had to get back to Enniskillen. But he was told later that when the area was given the all-clear, people actually came back to the shop in the hope of meeting him.'

Gordon and Joan received hundreds of letters from readers in all parts of the British Isles and beyond. Some, who were suffering a bereavement of their own, could only read a portion at a time, but they gained a great deal from sharing Gordon and Joan's experience. The fellowship of suffering and bereavement is one that unites and binds. The book had its own life and its own mission. Gordon and Joan both felt that it did a great deal of good. Peter, Ingrid and Julie Anne were also grateful for the book's simplicity and lack of sentimentality or sensationalism. It also meant that Marie had not been forgotten. Ever conscious that Marie's voice had been silenced by the bomb, through this book – somehow – her life was able to influence others.

One of Joan's favourite passages in the book was, and still is, Gordon's reference to a scribbled note of Marie's which was written just before she died. She was trying to deal with the kind of doubts we all have from time to time, and she wrote down 'My prayer', after studying the Epistle of James:

Thank you Lord, for your Word. Without you I, too, would be an orphan. Lord help me by bringing others to be blessed, also help me to grow in maturity and completeness, and receive the crown of life. Lord, my career is up-front in my mind at the moment, with Night Duty. Help me to listen to my patients and act on their problems. Lord, I pray for my great friends Mum and Dad, thank you for their love... 'JAWS' [Julie Anne]: please, Lord, be with her and especially Anne-Marie. I pray for Northern Ireland and the whole world. I pray for the church, that I may do my role. Thank you Lord. Give me wisdom.

Joan says: 'That was the voice of Marie which we wanted people to hear, when they thought of Enniskillen. Many people did hear that voice in the pages of the book, and that was a great comfort. You could really say that the whole experience of preparing for the book – thinking of it, talking it out and watching it take shape on paper – all these aspects were the making of Gordon. It brought him out of himself, it helped to focus his mind, it gave him a purpose and it also presented him with something in tangible form which he could take around the country, indeed around the British Isles. Once he had the book in his hand, or a pile in the back of the car, he really felt that his mission was beginning in earnest. There is one lovely story from Wales, about Customs Officials who were querying the contents of several boxes of the books which had been sent from Enniskillen and which were being collected by a clergyman at Holyhead. "Don't worry," he advised the Customs people. "I can assure you that there are no bombs in these boxes – these are boxes full of love and forgiveness."'

Gordon had emerged from his personal wilderness of suffering and pain in a much more confident frame of mind and with increasing strength to face the world. From the autumn of 1990, some three years after Marie's death, he was to undertake a punishing schedule of speaking engagements and public appearances, and although he did not yet know it, he was destined to play a significant part in Irish public life. The big draper from the small town of Enniskillen still had much to say, and a large number of people were still eager to listen.

9

The Public Speaker

The publication of the book was taken as a general signal that Gordon was willing and able to bring Marie's story to as wide an audience as possible, and the publicity surrounding its launch led to a steady stream of invitations to speak. That stream became a torrent when he was invited by the then Irish Premier, Albert Reynolds, to join the Irish Senate in 1993. It was an immensely punishing schedule which took a heavy toll of his emotions and energy. In the last years of his life, Gordon was so well known that he could hardly walk the streets of Dublin (or elsewhere) without being stopped and often given film-star treatment by total strangers. He loved to be recognized, but he was genuinely embarrassed by adulation, and he cringed when people referred to him as a 'saint'.

Even though he had qualities which were indeed saintly, it was Gordon's humour, charm and earthy practicality which bowled people over. His firm handshake and his wide smile confirmed that here indeed was a warm and vulnerable human being who also had great inner strength. He was also an accomplished public speaker who could hold an audience in rapt attention. He had a powerful story to tell, and he told it well. His simplicity in telling the story was riveting, and though he must have told Marie's story literally hundreds of times, he was still able to touch a raw, deep emotion, not only in those who were hearing him for the first time but also in those who had heard the story several times over.

Any lesser figure might have ended up by sounding banal and repetitive, but Gordon always told Marie's story with conviction and freshness, as if the nightmarish experience of the Enniskillen bomb had taken place only the day before. And he had the unique authority of someone who had been through a bomb-blast and had survived an explosion which had killed his beloved daughter and ten other people, as well as injuring more than three-score other innocent bystanders. No one ever dared to contradict the authority of this man, who had been at the centre of the utmost horror and had survived to tell the story as it was, in plain, stark terms – and yet with hope and love and forgiveness. Gordon Wilson made the rubble, the blood and the anguish as tangible and as real to every one of his listeners as the very platform or pulpit where he stood. It was as if he was reliving the experience over and over, and his profound sense of loss and his passionate desire that Marie's death should not have been in vain never failed to show through.

Often his voice faltered, and it seemed unlikely that he or his audience could avoid tears. But his inner strength always pulled him through, and he would often conclude his address to prolonged applause or, even more impressively, to stunned silence. John Turner, the President of Ballymena Rotary Club, wrote to Gordon thanking him for his visit, and he noted: 'The fact that no one wished to ask a question when you had finished was indicative of how deeply moved everyone was. It was obvious that your talk was born out of your own deep sorrow, and that is what made it so meaningful to us all. Thank you for coming, and for all that you said, and are.' He added a final revealing sentence: 'My only regret about your visit is that you paid for your own lunch! We never expect our guests to pay, but I sense that it will be no good remonstrating with you about this, nor about the expense you had in making the journey, so we accept it in the spirit of Rotary.'

Later that year, just two months before he died in 1995, Gordon spoke in Blackpool at the Annual Conference of Rotary International in Great Britain and Ireland. After the conference, the President, David Morgan, wrote: 'The standing ovation which you received (the only one given during Conference) was testimony to the delegates' appreciation, but I would not like the occasion to pass without recording my personal thanks to you for a message which fitted so perfectly into the morning's theme of Christian love.'

Gordon spoke in churches and chapels, abbeys and cathedrals, in schools and universities, in golf clubs and hotels, at Rotary meetings and on any and every occasion when he could tell Marie's story directly, or by his very presence at a gathering remind the audience of the pain of ordinary people and the depth of their suffering as a result of the Ulster Troubles. He was careful in his choice of engagements, though like every speaker, he accepted one or two which turned out to be only peripheral to his main mission. One of his shortcomings was in taking on too much, even when some of the requests for his presence or endorsement were well meant but hardly appropriate. However, he did have his own limits. One night, shortly after Marie died, he was telephoned by a man from New York who told him that he could 'make a million bucks' by taking Marie's story around the American speaking circuit. On another occasion he was asked if he would lend his name to a special trophy for a greyhound race. He resisted such blandishments with his customary humour and sound common sense.

Sometimes he was simply too busy to accept all the offers to speak. In his home at Cooper Crescent there is a large file of invitations which he had to decline, always regretfully. A typical letter of reply was the one which he wrote to the University of Limerick Debating Society: 'I regretfully have to refuse, because in that very same week I have accepted invitations to Belfast, Chester and Dublin.'

Joan began to see the toll it was beginning to take of him. He would always prepare carefully for any engagement, whether it was to open an art exhibition or to speak in a cathedral. Sometimes he would be tense before his speech, and unable to eat anything. Afterwards, more often than not, he would hardly have time to take a cup of tea, because of the crowds of people who wanted to meet him, to talk to him, to ask him to sign a copy of the book, or just to shake his hand. Usually it would take him a couple of days to recover, and by that time he was off again.

Joan hated him spending weekends away from home: 'I knew why he had to go, and invariably it was for a good reason, but he needed his weekends to rest and recuperate. I made it my business to try to make sure he spent weekends relaxing properly. I saw to it that he had proper food, rest and relaxation, and to be fair, he really did relax when he came home. He always said to me after he had been travelling for a few days, "It's great to get home to your own fireside and your own bed."

But when he was at home during the week, he was very businesslike. In spring and summer he liked to get up very early on the clear mornings, about 5.30 a.m., and go to his study to work on a speech or deal with mail to make it ready for his secretary, who came in at 9.30. I remember his almost boyish sense of achievement at getting up early and doing a good "day's" work while it was still morning.' Joan worried about his health and his stamina, but not about his ability to tell Marie's story to any audience in any place. She had known from their wedding day that he was a natural public speaker and loved an audience.

Despite Gordon's extensive list of engagements, Joan only heard Gordon tell Marie's story four times. She was still working full time as a teacher and could not accompany Gordon everywhere. She also felt that he could get through his list of engagements more quickly on his own. However, when she did hear him tell the story, it was so painful for her that she could hardly bear it:

'Gordon told it so well, but it affected me so deeply that it took me days to get over it. Julie Anne told me that it had the same effect on her. We said to one another, "This story is tearing each of us apart inside – what must it be doing to him?" I remember hearing him speak at a prize-giving for nurses at Altnagelvin Hospital. I knew that these young women identified with Marie, and as Gordon spoke to the nurses and their families and friends, you could have heard a pin drop. On another occasion we both addressed a group of women in Dublin, and afterwards they came up to talk to us. They were lovely, warm-hearted people, and several of them had lost a son or daughter at an early age due to a road accident or a premature death. These women taught us that many others were grieving, and that so many different people have to face so many challenges of their own. I think we learned a great deal from each other.'

Some occasions were particularly memorable, and in their own way enjoyable – such as Gordon and Joan's visit to Westminster Abbey on 4 July 1994 for the Annual Service of The Grey Coat Hospital, in the presence of pupils of Queen Anne's School, Caversham, Westminster City School, Emmanuel School and St Matthew's School. Joan was impressed by the Abbey's Jerusalem Chamber, where Henry IV died, where the King James Bible was compiled, and where the Queen dines once a year. This kind of visit boosted Joan's spirits. She loves music and art, and this kind of 'normality' – like that experienced by any tourist on a visit to London – helped to take her mind off other things.

Though Gordon liked to portray himself as 'the wee draper from the wee town of Enniskillen', he was anything but that. He knew that he was a good public speaker, and he enjoyed it – though his message drained him emotionally each time he delivered it. He was happy to share the same platform with others, but he found it difficult to take a back seat if the subject was Marie Wilson. Joan recalls a meeting in Edinburgh at which she was due to address a large audience of Scottish women: 'I was nervous enough about the prospect of speaking to them, but I also had to contend with Gordon, who was a bit miffed that he had not been invited to speak, and "wondered" if he might say a few words when I had finished. I loved him and I admired him, but I had no illusions about him – he was a real old chauvinist at heart!' Gordon loved an audience and he could see no point in not speaking when he had come so far. Besides, he could never be 'Joan Wilson's husband', although he was perfectly content to be known as 'Marie Wilson's dad'.

Like every good speaker, Gordon knew the value of humour. People who came to hear him for the first time were rightly expecting a serious, even searing, address – but they might not have expected the joke or humorous quip with which he usually began. A typical example was the story he told to a very large audience in York, on the last major public engagement before he died. Here is what he said, taken almost verbatim from a recording of his speech:

This is a true story of a colleague of mine in the Irish Senate, by the name of Senator Fergal Quinn. You've probably never heard of him, but he is the 'boss-man' of a chain of grocery supermarkets in Ireland, a sort of 'Sainsbury's of Ireland'. He went on a motoring holiday with his wife last year to America, and he tells the story that every day on his journey he passed a particular grocery supermarket, or another branch of it, and underneath the name in every case they said, 'The friendliest supermarkets in

America'. On every window there were posters that said, 'If our checkout girl does not say, "Thank you", we'll give you back a dollar.'

Fergal said to his wife, 'I like that. I'm going to try that when I get back to Ireland.' And she said, 'For goodness sake, you're on your holidays! Forget about business.' He said, 'Never mind. I like that. That's good.' On the very last day, on the way back to the airport, he passed one of the stores, and he went in and bought something he didn't need – a throw-away razor costing 1 dollar and 35 cents. He went to the girl at the checkout desk, his wife beside him afraid that he was going to start the Third World War! And he gave her a 5-dollar bill. She took the bill, and she took the razor, and she put the razor into a bag, and she gave him back 3 dollars and 65 cents change, and she said, 'Next, please.' And he said, 'Sorry, but haven't you made a mistake?'

So she took the razor back and she took the change back, and she put the whole thing through the till again, and she gave him back the razor, and she gave him back the change, and she said, 'No sir, there's no mistake. Next, please.' And he said, 'I think you owe me a dollar.' And she said, 'Oh no, sir. That offer finished yesterday!'

A wave of sustained laughter rippled through the audience, but almost in the next breath Gordon went on to talk about his early life in Enniskillen, and about the explosion and its aftermath.

Gordon was particularly good at relating to young people. The letters file in his study contains many tributes to this particular skill. For example, Gillian Wharton (the assistant curate at St Paul's Church, Glenageary, County Dublin, where Gordon addressed an audience of young people) wrote, in a letter describing the impression he had made: 'The impact of your story was, and is, amazing. I say "is", because people are still talking about it.' Gordon spoke to a very wide range of schools, from Omagh Academy and St Louis Grammar School, Kilkeel, in Northern Ireland, to St Vincent's Secondary School and North Presentation Secondary School in County Cork, and many places in between. The students at St Vincent's wrote this to Gordon:

Thank you for showing us, through your actions, what it is to forgive and to struggle for peace and reconciliation. It is through your example and the example of like-minded people, that the light of peace is held up, giving us all hope. For the gift of hope, we thank you.

Some of the most revealing reactions came from the pupils of North Presentation College, who were asked to describe their feelings about Gordon's visit. Here are some of the comments which they wrote:

When you spoke on Friday, there was no hate or revenge in your voice, but love and sincerity. I felt ashamed to be in your presence. *(Mary Condon)*

Your lovely story brought memories of my sister who died this year. She would be six the week you came. I wouldn't know everything you felt because Marie was your daughter – but I know how it feels to lose someone very close. *(Caroline Kelleher)*

As you spoke, I had tears in my eyes, but yet I had hope in my heart. *(Gwen McHale)*

The message I learned was that no matter what people do to you, still pray for them. *(Ellen Quillegan)*

I couldn't help feeling proud touching the hand that was holding Marie Wilson's as they were underneath the rubble. *(Tricia O'Keefe)*

I believe that your gentle, loving and forgiving character will bring the communities in Northern Ireland together. I pray for more people like you. *(Caroline McFadden)*

The Principal, Sister Kathleen Quinlan, recalls that day: 'Peace was his dream. As we gathered in the Gym hall and listened to him telling the story of Marie with such passion and emotion we, too, cried. No anger, no revenge – only a cry for peace from his heart. He was an inspiration, and we fondly look at his pictures and letter to us hanging on our wall. He was a truly great man and we are so proud that he visited our school.'

Gordon Wilson's appeal to young people crossed all the divides and national boundaries. Following his visit to the Greensward School in Hockley, Essex, there was a report in a local newspaper. It quoted a pupil, Amy Ensum, who had heard him speak the previous day. Amy said: 'Some of the time I feel quite guilty that we don't really think about the people because they are so far away. Mr Wilson made it feel more personal. You would think that he would want revenge, but he was so calm and said he totally forgave them. If he can forgive people for something like that, petty arguments don't seem so important.'

Gordon also visited Grangemouth High School, roughly halfway between Stirling and Edinburgh. Ian Cranston, a teacher, has warm memories of the visit: 'He arrived in the school, and after a half-hour's chat, I took him to speak to two classes of sixteen-year-olds and a few staff. He talked for an hour about Marie's story, and you can imagine the effect on the pupils and staff.'

That evening, Gordon spoke to an audience of some 400 people in the Town Hall at Grangemouth. Ian particularly remembers his easy conversation from the platform with a group of Irish people in the audience, and his gentle, relaxed humour with the chairman, Harry Pope. Later he signed a large number of copies of the book. Ian recalls: 'The ground that he helped us to walk upon that day was holy ground indeed. What most do I remember of Gordon? I guess it was the story he chose to tell – a "love" story, a lovely story, and yet a sad story. For himself, a person who lived on the risky side of faith, and was willing to pay the price of that costly peace-making. He was a man who gave what he had to give. Can you tell me how someone I met for one afternoon and evening could matter so much? I grieved for a Peter I never knew, and for a widow I've still to meet.'

Eryl Edwards, a social worker from Bala in Gwynedd, encouraged his Sunday school class in 1987 to write individual notes of sympathy to Gordon, who, characteristically, sent letters of reply. Gordon and Eryl became friends. On three occasions Gordon visited Wales – in 1993 for a six-day visit to Dolgellau, Bala, Aberystwyth, Porthmadog, Pwllheli, Caernarfon and Bangor. The next year he visited Swansea and Carmarthen, and in 1995 Mold, Tywyn and Cemaes in Anglesey. He spoke in churches and schools, to great effect. Amy Ogden, aged thirteen, from Ysgol Eifionydd, Porthmadog, recalled: 'If I were to describe Mr Wilson in one word, I would say that he was a very determined man, totally devoted to his cause and willing to go to any extent to fulfil his ambitions. Even though he has now passed away, his memory is still in my heart and he is a role model for each and every one of us.' Lowri Davies, aged fourteen, of Ysgol Gyfun Gwyr, wrote: 'Gordon Wilson was the bravest man I have ever met, travelling around Britain, relating his story and trying to make sure that this sort of thing never happens again.'

Gordon's sincerity shone through, but so did his humour. Eryl Edwards remembers that he had trouble pronouncing the Welsh place-names, and he said that Bala was the only town in Wales which he could pronounce properly! Eryl recalls: 'Gordon made such an impact on me and the people of Wales that, following Peter's death, I remember him telling me that he received more letters and cards from Wales than any other country in the world. It was an honour and a privilege to have met such a Christian and to have enjoyed his company.'

Gordon was always delighted to meet Ulster folk when he was speaking outside Northern Ireland, and he usually made a point of finding time to talk with them. Maddy Tongue, an Ulsterwoman who moved to Cambridge some months earlier, recalls meeting Gordon in the spring of 1995 when he came to speak at a local church which had a particularly sad connection with the Ulster Troubles. The minister, David Armstrong, had left Northern Ireland some time before because of what he felt were unreasonable and unbearable pressures on people like him, who were trying to bridge the sectarian divide.

Maddy Tongue remembers: 'Gordon began his talk with the background into which Marie was born. It was all so foreign to the people in that gathering. He spoke with a dignity and a pride in being Irish, and I shared his pride in that Cambridge church. His gentle jokes about the absurdities and contradictions of life in Northern Ireland got no reaction from his attentive English audience, unused to our way – with humour alongside death and horror. He did not compromise or cut short his telling of Marie's story, but shared with us each agonizing moment of that awful time. Gordon stunned us with his humanity, and exhausted us with the agony. And afterwards, as I spoke to him, his eyes lit up, firstly at the accent, and secondly when he learned that my husband was a conductor under whom Marie had played the violin, with the Studio Symphony Orchestra in Belfast, and it was a happy period for her.'

Gordon became so well known as a bridge-builder that he was frequently asked to take part in different kinds of religious services and gatherings. He spent much time in preparing his addresses for such occasions, and his hard work, experience and spiritual insight shone through. One of his last contributions was given in a television programme on Good Friday 1995, under the auspices of the Tullamore and Dungannon Faith Communities, in association with Radio Telefis Eireann and Ulster Television. He was one of a number of speakers, and his short meditation demonstrated his ability to say a great deal in a few words:

'And Jesus cried with a loud voice, "Father, into your hands I commend my spirit."'

The experience of bereavement and injury through the troubles of the past 25 years has for me, and I feel sure for many others, been felt as an experience of abandonment by God. Often we have asked, 'What has God's purpose been in all of this?' Why has he forsaken us? There are still days when we ask these questions and others like them. And I still have not found an answer.

When we suffer, it seems as though God is absent. Jesus thought that when he cried, 'My God, why hast thou forsaken me?' It was then, perhaps, that he realized, even though he was suffering and dying (suffering and dying for you and me), that God was not absent, but was present in his suffering and in his dying. God had been there all the time.

Being human means we will know suffering, or lose someone close to us, and, in time, face our own death. God did not make us in a way which would leave us free from such things. These final words of Jesus, 'Father, into your hands I commend my spirit', tell us that at such times we have not been abandoned by God, but that he is with us, seeing us through the suffering and the dying.

In the eighth chapter of his letter to the Romans, Paul speaks of the power of the love of God. For those whose way is committed unto God, he concludes in those wonderful final verses by saying that nothing 'will be able to separate us from the love of God which is in Christ Jesus our Lord'.

To know that nothing can separate us from the love of God which is in Christ Jesus has been our hope in adversity, our strength at times of weakness and our confidence when we felt abandoned by God.

In the face of our loss, pain, despair and our greatest adversity, these final words of Jesus show us that all we can do, and all we ought to do, is to place ourselves in his care, to commend ourselves unto him.

Gordon's impact that evening is remembered by Pat Gallagher, a member of the Irish Parliament who represents the area. He recalls:

My abiding memory is that of the queue of people who lined up after the Service to meet Gordon and to shake his hand. It took nearly half an hour, and I realized the impression he had made on the ordinary people of Ireland.

It is almost impossible to estimate the good that Gordon Wilson achieved through his many speeches and public appearances. But there can be no doubt about the enormous price he paid physically and emotionally in bringing Marie's story to the world. This price was starkly illustrated by the opening words of his address at the Christian Renewal

Centre in Rostrevor on 10 July 1994. He had been travelling for several days on speaking engagements, and it showed. His wounds were never far from the surface, and he was very tired. He began his main address with these words:

> I haven't slept in my own bed for seven nights. I've been in four capital cities in the past five days and I've spoken in every one of them. The last week has been rough, but when I get home tonight, I am on my holidays. If I look tired tonight, it is because I *am* tired. I get invitations to come and talk from all over the place... on subjects like grief, tolerance or reconciliation, forgiveness or peace. And I say 'No'. But I say, 'I will come and tell you the story of Marie Wilson, about her life and her death, and what I call the aftermath'...I propose to tell you a story – Marie's story. I think it's a love story, a lovely story, and certainly a story of love. For me, of course, it has to be and still is a sad story, and you will understand why. And so, if the odd time my voice breaks, or you see a tear in my eye, I'd like to think you will understand. It still hurts – of course it does. And every time I tell the story...I say, 'This is not the story of Enniskillen. This is *a* story *from* Enniskillen', and in saying this I do not forget ten other lovely, gentle people who died in that bomb, and that now nearly three and a half thousand people in Northern Ireland are in their graves, as a result of the Troubles.

Towards the end of his address he revealed the secret of his strength:

> Gradually I have come to terms, within my limitations, with life, and I can be as private or as public as I want to be, or I am able to be. I know I can never be the same man again – no one ever can be who loses a loved one in the Troubles. And I have not been led down the avenues of getting involved with parties or movements or groups. I have tried to tell the story of Marie Wilson, and through it all my faith has been strengthened. I am sure of God's love for me, and of my need to love him, because only in his love can we have hope and reconciliation, and peace.

As in so much of Gordon Wilson's life and witness, his words spoke for themselves, but out of all the many tributes and letters of praise and thanks from those who heard him speak, one stands out. It comes from Carol O'Brien, a schoolgirl in County Cork, who heard him address her class. She wrote: 'I learned an important lesson on Friday: it's to forgive. As soon as I went home I went over to my friend's house, which I didn't do for two months. She came out, and I hugged her – and now we're best friends again – but we wouldn't be if you didn't come.'

Out of his tragedy, suffering and despair, Gordon Wilson, with the help of God, created something fragile yet immensely strong, and something that was and remains truly beautiful.

10

The Politician

In February 1993 Gordon Wilson received an invitation from Albert Reynolds, then the Irish Prime Minister, to accept a seat in the Irish Senate. One of Reynolds' advisers, Dr Martin Mansergh, phoned Gordon with the offer and gave him only 24 hours to think it over, due to the pressure of politics. Both he and Joan were taken completely by surprise, but it was the kind of offer that would come only once in a lifetime. It was an invitation which caused Gordon much heart-searching, in the limited time he was given to make up his mind. He knew that if he accepted, his decision would be misunderstood by many of his Protestant friends and acquaintances in Fermanagh and other parts of Northern Ireland, who would accuse him of betraying Unionism by taking a seat in the Upper House of the Irish Parliament in Dublin. Such people regarded the Republic of Ireland as a foreign country.

On the other hand, Gordon and Joan both knew that this was an opportunity for the message of Enniskillen, with its emphasis on forgiveness and reconciliation, to reach a wider audience throughout Ireland and beyond. An acceptance of Albert Reynolds' offer would in itself be a practical demonstration of cross-border neighbourliness.

The whole Wilson family discussed it, and Gordon contacted a number of friends to seek their advice. He knew that he would be criticized in public, but the offer challenged him, and a seat in the Senate would bring him back to his roots in Dublin, a city in which he had gone to school and which he had always liked. It was crucial, however, that Joan should approve, since such an appointment would mean spending a lot of time away from home, in addition to the time he already spent on speaking engagements to tell 'the Marie story'.

Joan and the family encouraged him to accept the offer. She knew that it would take great courage on his part, but that he would do a good job. 'His presence in Dublin would be a constant reminder of what had happened in Enniskillen. Even if Gordon never opened his mouth in the Senate, he would be making a point, just by being there.' In the event, the Senate was the making of him. 'They gave him a wonderful, warm welcome and greeted him with open arms. The Senate gave him a new lease of life.'

Gordon went to Dublin to see Albert Reynolds, before he made up his mind. He told the Premier (or Taoiseach) that he thought of himself as an ordinary, humble man and that he could not understand why he was being considered for a seat in the Senate. Reynolds assured him that he would not be expected to vote for the Government and that he would be totally independent. Reynolds told him: 'I just want you to be a voice for reconciliation and forgiveness in the Senate, and on any occasion which might advance that process.'

Albert Reynolds was delighted that Gordon was willing to accept. When the vacancy arose in the Senate, he had looked around for someone who personified peace and reconciliation. He said: 'I was looking more to the North than the South, because I wanted to further the process of reconciliation up there. Gordon Wilson's name immediately stood out. He was head and shoulders above everyone else. I didn't know him personally, but his reputation had gone before him.'

The appointment was not without its critics in the South, some of whom looked on it as a typical political gimmick by Albert Reynolds. Emily O'Reilly, then the political correspondent of the now-defunct *Irish Press* newspaper, expressed her misgivings and echoed those of others when she noted that Gordon symbolized 'political transcendence, forgiveness, reconciliation and morality on a level few of us could ever hope to reach. However, the day he makes his first "political" speech on Northern policy, will be the day he ceases to exist as the symbol he is now.' It was greatly to Gordon's credit that he did achieve the difficult balance between speaking about vexed political subjects such as the North and retaining what the *Irish Press* headline-writer called 'The very "Gordon Wilsonness" of Gordon Wilson'.

He proved the sceptics wrong, not only by the force and uniqueness of his personality, but also by the way in which he operated politically. Albert Reynolds comments that Gordon was not a 'good politician' in the traditional sense of someone who has to operate within strict parameters and toe the party line. 'He would do and say what he believed was for the best, and some people might have said, "A good politician would not have done that", but the thought never entered Gordon's mind. He reminded me of the words of Eleanor Roosevelt who said that politicians should do things which politicians think they cannot do. Gordon was one of those politicians.'

His first speech in the Senate was delivered on 25 March 1993, five days after the Warrington bomb and four days after his public challenge to the IRA to meet him face to face. His speech was powerful, emotional and well reasoned, and it showed his many listeners in the Chamber and elsewhere the calibre of the man. His opening words set out his credentials, his philosophy and his purpose clearly. He said: 'I welcome this opportunity to speak today from my heart. I speak knowing that God is good, and that God is love. I speak not in my strength but in his. I speak for myself, and I speak as Marie Wilson's Dad.' He was not afraid to show his emotions. 'I hope that I do not look as nervous as I feel. I hope I can control my emotions because Northern Ireland, and all of Ireland and its people are close to my heart, and we are bleeding to death.' He also referred to his recent attempts to make contact with the IRA. And he told the Senate, 'The IRA is composed of human beings like ourselves and they have suffered too, just as we have at their expense.' Within a very short time, Gordon Wilson was making his mark.

His maiden speech was an impassioned plea for reconciliation and for a change of heart, and he urged people to communicate more in order to be aware of one another's difficulties. He talked about a 'huge gulf' of unreality which was keeping people apart, and which could never be bridged by political logic and political action alone. He said: 'Without a healing of wounds and a change of heart, this gulf will not be bridged, there will not be a fresh start, a reawakening of what is good in Ireland, a rebirth of hope that must travel some day like a torch held aloft to all four corners of our strife-torn land.' And he ended by quoting the Prayer of St Francis of Assisi: 'Lord, make me an instrument of your peace.'

It was a remarkable speech from a man who had never been in politics and who had spent most of his life working as a draper in a small town. Austin Currie, an Ulsterman who was making his own mark in the Dail (the Lower House) as a bright and able politician and who was appreciative of and helpful to Gordon, said privately that after his maiden speech in the Senate, Gordon's reputation soared. People had expected to find in their midst a good and a serious man who had tragically lost a daughter in a bomb-blast, but they had not expected someone who, when he spoke, made everyone sit up and listen, and who gave fresh urgency and poignancy to the search for peace.

His immense moral authority impressed everyone, not only in the Senate but later on in the Forum for Peace and Reconciliation which was set up in Dublin by the Irish Government, following the Provisional IRA ceasefire on 31 August 1994. In the opening words of its Chairperson, Judge Catherine McGuinness, its purpose was to examine ways in which 'lasting peace, stability and reconciliation can be established among all the people of Ireland, and on the steps required to remove barriers of distrust, on the basis of promoting respect for the equal rights and validity of both traditions and identities.' The Forum first met on 28 October 1994, and was supported by the major parties in the Republic and Northern Ireland, who sent representatives to its regular Friday meetings. It was also supported by Sinn Fein, whose delegates mixed freely with politicians from the mainline and smaller parties. But from the start, the work of the Forum was boycotted by the Northern Unionist parties, a development which significantly diminished its effectiveness, and reduced it, in the opinion of some observers, to a mere talking-shop.

However, it carried out valuable work, mainly as a sounding-board between Southern and Northern politicians (except the Unionists) and Sinn Fein. A drafting committee under Judge McGuinness spent many hours producing a document entitled 'Paths to a Political Settlement: Realities, Principles and Requirements'. Sinn Fein were unable to agree to a key recommendation that the right of self-determination of the

Irish people should be subject to the consent of a majority in Northern Ireland. Though Gordon died several months before the document was produced, he had played an important role not only as a member of the drafting committee but also in the plenary sessions, where his reputation for straight talking and for uncommon common sense was further enhanced.

As an independent, he had no party back-up, but he did have the services of a secretary-assistant named Aisling Maguire, whom he regarded highly. She and others helped him to draft his speeches, but the thrust of the arguments, like the content, was his own. He was meticulous about punctuation and grammar, and as he outlined his desired content verbally, he paced up and down, and sometimes ended with the spiritual fervour of an old-style preacher. He was not afraid to use strong, emotive and highly personal language. In his first speech to the Forum, like that to the Senate, he held his listeners spell-bound. He said: 'When you have stood at an open grave and laid to rest "bone of your bone and flesh of your flesh", it adds, not only a poignancy to it all, but an urgency to seeking peace – not just a temporary cessation of warfare, but a permanent reality for all people everywhere. There has been too much blood shed in this land, too many bodies bruised, and too many hearts broken for us not to call a permanent halt to it all.'

He ended his speech by saying, 'Love is enough.' He said: 'If that sounds naively simple, let's try it out, because we have travelled other roads, and we can see where they have brought us. Love it must be, but love in action, spelt out and worked out in strategies for peace and reconciliation.'

People on all sides spoke appreciatively in private not only of his moral authority but also of his practical, no-nonsense approach in dealing with people. Judge McGuinness remembered that he was able to bring people down to earth when they began to embark on flights of fancy. 'He would say to them, "This simply won't work."' He also had a calming effect when political disagreements began to turn into heated argument. Gordon's speeches were short, to the point and full of meaning. 'Everything meant something. Everyone listened to him, not only because of who he was but also because of what he was. He was an extraordinary character.' Even those who were sceptical and cynical did not dispute his sincerity or his emotional power.

Gordon sometimes liked to portray himself as a naive politician, but he fooled no one. Seamus Mallon, Deputy Leader of the Social Democratic Labour Party, recalls his disarming way of telling people that he knew nothing about politics, and then proceeding to give a most impressive display of political acumen. Mr Mallon comments, 'He was the most "non-political" politician I have ever met.' Austin Currie at first thought that Gordon might be an innocent in the hard world of politics. 'Then he told me that he was naive, and I realized that he was not so naive after all! He was very shrewd, and a great deal shrewder than some people gave him credit for.'

He was, in fact, an able politician, not so much in the traditional sense of being a party man, but more as a political operator who knew where the levers of power were situated and how to use them. Senior figures at the Forum used to smile at the way in which he kept mentioning Fermanagh in his speeches, like an old-style politician looking for votes. And he made sure that his local newspapers, including the splendidly named *Impartial Reporter*, were sent copies of all his speeches.

In his earlier days he had chosen deliberately to stay out of politics, but the experience in the Senate and Forum many years later gave him the opportunity to show that he indeed had considerable political flair. (This begs the question: What might have developed in the Northern Ireland of pre-Troubles days if a whole generation of liberals like Gordon Wilson had not opted out of politics?)

Noel Dempsey, a well-known member of the Irish Parliament, was another confidant of Gordon's, and he had recommended Gordon to Albert Reynolds earlier on. He found Gordon 'a thorough gentleman, a Christian gentleman, a gentle soul, aware of the complexities of the political situation in which he found himself, and yet beautifully innocent and naive in many matters political.'

Gordon was a canny operator who knew what he was doing. Professor Tom Garvin, Head of the Politics Department at University College Dublin, helped him with some of his speeches. He believes that Gordon was remarkable, tough-minded and humane. 'He was also a wily old bird, who could use his situation to great political effect. He would ask the same question continually, in part out of genuine pain, in part out of steely political purpose: "Why did they kill my Marie?"' Gordon believed that Providence had put him in a key position to bring about peace and dialogue in Ireland, and he felt duty-bound to use it to the limit.

He was able to say things that others could not say. His utterances and speeches sometimes had the ring of an Old Testament prophet. In a world of increasing secularism, he was not afraid to bring metaphysics into politics. There was more to life, he believed, than the intellect. There were emotions too, and the inner life of the spirit. Dr John Robb, a surgeon from Ballymoney in Northern Ireland, who was a former Senator himself in Dublin, was one of Gordon's valued confidants. He says: 'The cerebral approach on its own will not solve the Irish problem unless there is also a movement of the spirit. Gordon gave a lead on this. When he spoke at the Forum or in the Senate he was not trying to score political points. He was pointing out central truths. It was the real Gordon Wilson, not a political figure, who was speaking.' Gordon was driven by a terrible anguish, but was totally prepared to be his own man. He was able to talk to people at their level and engage them in a way that few others were able to do. 'He never claimed to be a politician's politician, but he tried to move people by holding aloft a realization that there could be different way, a non-adversarial way of solving political problems.'

Gordon valued the counsel of Dr John Alderdice, leader of the Alliance Party in Northern Ireland, whom he met regularly in the Forum. He called him affectionately 'Doctor John'. Alderdice feels that at times Gordon's stance on issues was almost a reproach to the 'professional' politicians. 'He drew you away from the politics and always brought you back to the principles. He believed that if he wanted to bring out the best in people, he had to address what was best in them. If people thought him foolish for doing this, it did not worry him.'

Gordon was no fool, and yet he retained his endearing quality of innocence, which some people thought to be naivety. He believed deeply that if people really had the love of God in their hearts, they would be able to live peacefully in what he called 'this corner of God's garden'. When Aisling Maguire told him that she was an atheist, he was taken aback. 'Are there many of you about?' he asked her teasingly, with his famous, broad grin. Aisling says: 'I admired him enormously and I never for one moment felt that he was other-worldly. He was much too shrewd and down to earth for that. But he had a romantic view that 95% of the people in the Republic were devout Catholics. He did not want to know or to accept that when many of them heard the 6.00 p.m. Angelus on Irish television, they took it as a signal to set their watches rather than as a spiritual check!' Even on some personal matters he was blind, or chose to turn a blind eye. Michelle Kennedy, his part-time secretary in Enniskillen, had a mind of her own, and she told him one day in exasperation how stubborn he was. Gordon was amazed, and talked about it for weeks. Joan told Michelle that it was the best thing she had ever said to him.

Gordon had expected criticism for taking his seat in the Senate and for participating in the Forum, and he certainly received it. Raymond Ferguson, a Unionist councillor who often shared morning coffee with Gordon and his other friends in Enniskillen, was fully aware of the courage he showed by going to Dublin. 'He was a good Unionist who put forward their point of view, but he was misunderstood by those Unionists in Fermanagh and elsewhere who immediately suspect anyone who pays too much attention to Dublin. However, he might have been naive in believing that the views he wanted to impart would not be criticized to the degree they were. Maybe he took himself a bit too seriously at times. Criticism did not seem to run off him like it did off other people.'

He was misunderstood not only by his political critics but also by some friends and acquaintances. Mary Harney, leader of the Progressive Democrats, was another of his confidants in Dublin. She says: 'Some people told him, "Gordon, when you're in Dublin, don't trust them. You can't trust Catholics." That reaction amazed him, as did the fact that many of his friends never even mentioned his seat in the Senate or his work for the Forum. It wasn't discussed – no congratulations, nothing. He wasn't surprised that some people disapproved so strongly that they could not even bring themselves to discuss it with him.'

Crawford Little, a long-time friend from Enniskillen, said that Gordon was aware that some people would take their business elsewhere because of what he had said and done, and he was hurt that this should be so. 'He did not endear himself to the strong right wing by accepting his seat on the Senate. To some of them, that was tantamount to going over to the enemy.' Others, however, recognized that he had acted from the best of motives. Crawford Little says: 'People like me, who had taken hardly any interest in the Senate previously, began to realize through Gordon's presence there that such a body existed, and that so much good could be done – which Gordon certainly did.'

Gordon and Joan were both sensitive to the criticisms. Joan says: 'It was not so much what people said, but, in some cases, what they did not say which was so telling. Some would chat to me, with Gordon standing beside me, but they would never mention his work in the Senate or the Forum. It was very obvious.' Others praised Gordon to his face, but talked about him behind his back. He knew who they were and what they said, for their words usually got back to him. One day two middle-aged women were in the shop, when they noticed Gordon talking to two nuns on the pavement outside. One of the women was overheard to say, 'Why doesn't he go back with those nuns to Dublin, where he belongs?' Though criticism hurt him, he did not apologize for his views. He was a determined man, and when he made up his mind, it was made up.

Some of the severest criticism came when he told the Forum that, in his opinion, a united Ireland would come, some day. He noted that Albert Reynolds could not see it coming in his lifetime, and that many Unionists and Protestants in Northern Ireland would welcome that statement from the former Irish Prime Minister, because it removed their fear that they would be dragged into to a united Ireland overnight against their wishes. In the meantime, he said, politicians must decide on a form of government to which all the people of Northern Ireland could be loyal. 'They must devise an interim structure or administration on the way to a united Ireland. It seems to me that the Irish Government has a responsibility to persuade the Unionist and Protestant people of Northern Ireland that their best future is in a united Ireland. This will not be easy, but it must be done.'

This radical statement required considerable courage, because a large number of Gordon's fellow-Protestants in the North regarded it as a heresy. This inevitably attracted newspaper headlines such as 'Bomb tragedy Dad backs united Ireland' and 'United Ireland will happen eventually – Wilson believes'. Many of his friends were furious, but he was putting forward a view held by some Protestants who believed that, given political and social stability and a guarantee of the same living standards in the North as existed under British rule, an all-Ireland settlement might be the best option in the long run. This view was discussed round many a middle-class dinner table, but it was not enunciated in public. Gordon Wilson was saying in public what some people were only half-daring to admit to themselves in private.

Many of his Dublin friends welcomed the fact that Gordon could express the Unionists' views so clearly, even if he travelled much further along the road to an all-Ireland concept than most other Unionists, who would never and could never bring themselves to accept such an idea. Few people in the South really understood the Unionist viewpoint, and they were regarded as a dour, ungracious bunch who could only parrot the old political war-cry of 'No Surrender'. Gordon was a welcome change, a civilized, witty man who knew how the Unionists thought and felt. But he chose not to allow himself to be boxed in as a 'typical' Unionist, and he retained the right, in the words of Aisling Maguire, 'to examine the fault-lines of his own society'.

It was no surprise, therefore, that Gordon was criticized and misunderstood, and that he received no support or thanks from Unionists. But to his dying day he regretted that the Unionists had so little self-confidence that they would not come to the Forum in Dublin to argue their case. He understood them, but they exasperated him. As best he could, he presented a liberal face of Unionism in Dublin, but he knew that there was no substitute for the presence of the established Unionist parties. His Dublin colleagues sympathized with his predicament. Paddy Harte, a Fine Gael member of the Irish Parliament from Donegal, was close to Gordon. He kept in touch with Northern Protestants and believed that many of them silently recognized Gordon's courage and honesty but could not admit this in public. 'To do so was to concede that they had to change.' Some, of course, did not listen to Gordon at all, and dismissed him completely.

Gordon was not a politician in the accepted sense, but he left a deep impression on politicians of every rank in Dublin, not only by what he said, but also by the way in which he said it. He had supreme moral authority, he had insight, he had impressive communication skills, and he had warmth and humour. Senator John Dardis, who was close to Gordon and who often spoke directly after him at the Senate, believes that one of his greatest strengths was his ability to mobilize the middle ground of politics. Because of the adversarial nature of politics, it is often difficult for the middle ground to find an audience, to create a space in the media. 'Gordon found that space because of who he was and what he was, and he used it superbly.' He was also acutely aware that in the Troubles people had been blown to bits and families had been totally shattered. 'There is a tendency in politics to treat a major incident of violence as a kind of abstract barbarity, but Gordon never forgot the human aspect of people whose lives were torn apart. He really felt for them.'

Albert Reynolds said that if Gordon had turned down his offer of a seat in the Senate he would not have known where to turn next. 'He was a man with a message and he did not have to respond to situations in the same way as politicians do. He was a free agent. I would never have got anyone else to fill that Senate post the way he filled it.' Judge Catherine McGuinness says that when Gordon died she and some senior civil servants sat down together to ask themselves whether Gordon's place at the Forum could or should be filled. They very quickly realized that it would be impossible to do so. 'There was just no one who could begin to fill the sort of place Gordon had filled. He was appointed because he was a special person, and there was simply no point in looking for someone else to fill the gap. We missed him terribly.'

Senator John Dardis made one of the most perceptive points of all: 'The Enniskillen bomb catapulted Gordon into prominence, but if he had not been the person he was, he would have sunk back into obscurity. A lot of people have said similar sorts of things after atrocities, but nobody has said them as well. Gordon was a very unusual person to begin with, but he didn't think he was. That was the mark of the man. None of us here who met him will ever forget him or the contribution he made.'

Gordon and Julie Anne on her wedding day

Peter, Ingrid, Eloise and Judith
at Julie Anne's wedding

Gordon and Joan at Julie
Anne's wedding

Peter, Eloise and Judith

Peter and Ingrid

Gordon with Julie Anne and his grandson, Scott
(Courtesy of the *Daily Mirror*)

Ingrid, Joan, Gordon, Eloise and Judith on cruise in the Caribbean after
Peter's death

Gordon with his grandson, Timothy

Gordon with the Queen at Westminster Abbey in 1995

Gordon outside the Irish Parliament building. This is one of Joan's favourite pictures. (Courtesy of RTE Guide)

Gordon at the Cenotaph in Enniskillen

11

The 'Spirit of Enniskillen'

'...I know there has to be a plan. It's part of a greater plan, and God is good. And we shall meet again.'

Gordon's words in that unforgettable interview on the night of Marie's death bore spontaneous witness to a deeply held Christian belief that God is in control and that out of the greatest evil, good can and will eventually come. He had no way of knowing how this would happen, but he was confident in his hope. Later on he defined what he had meant: 'It's not such much that good can come out of evil, but rather, in the case of Enniskillen and elsewhere, love can and will triumph over hatred.'

Despite the terrible suffering of those who were injured or had lost loved ones, the outreach and the bridge-building that took place directly as a result of the Enniskillen explosion did show that good and love could prevail, however heinous the evil and the hatred. The outpouring of heartfelt sympathy to all the victims and their families, and the desire of so many people to do something positive, were manifestations of the world-wide revulsion at such slaughter and carnage, and of a determination to create a society where such an outrage could not happen again.

Gordon felt that one of the good things to emerge from Enniskillen was that hatred was not allowed to triumph. In the period after the explosion there were widespread fears of reprisals against Roman Catholics by Loyalist paramilitaries, but these did not occur. Gordon's widely reported words set the tone for restraint and calm.

One of the immediate and practical results of the explosion was the establishment of an Appeal Fund, which was the idea of Gerry Burns, who was then Clerk and Chief Executive of Fermanagh District Council. He had been receiving floods of phone calls from people who asked how they could help, and he felt that the setting up of an Appeal Fund would help people to express their sympathy. The response was overwhelming, with donations coming from all parts of the United Kingdom and the Irish Republic, and from places as far apart as Vancouver and Pakistan, and from elsewhere, often from Fermanagh people who were living in various parts of the world.

A Board of Trustees was established, representing the four main churches and the two major political groups in the area, and a panel of specialists was set up to advise on claims. A total of around £660,000 was raised, and some 80% of this was given to the families of the injured and the bereaved. Some money was set aside for a permanent memorial, and for the establishment of an Enniskillen Youth and Community Trust, to help people from both communities to support events and activities for the elderly, the sick and the lonely.

The Marie Wilson Memorial Fund was the idea of Mary Riddell, then a feature writer with the *Daily Mirror*. The Fund was organized by the newspaper, and the idea touched its readers' hearts. Some £35,000 was raised, and this was distributed in various ways, bearing in mind that Marie had been a student nurse. Some £5,000 was sent to the Royal College of Nursing, and £2,500 to the Erne Hospital. Some of the money was used in the Royal Victoria Hospital, Belfast to furnish a special room for the relatives of seriously ill patients. It was called the Livingstone Room, in memory of a local surgeon, and Gordon and Joan donated a painting. The artist was Marie Prenter, the wife of one of Gordon's golfing companions, Joe Prenter. The balance of the Fund was used to help fund research scholarships for nurses.

The Rotary Clubs in Great Britain and Ireland raised nearly £20,000, and this was given to the Erne Hospital to help furnish two rooms – one for the relatives of patients, and one for the hospital's chaplains, who previously had to organize their business in someone else's office or, on occasions, in the hospital corridors. In all kinds of ways, large and little, people were showing how much they had abhorred the evil of the Enniskillen bomb and how much they longed for a time when the agony of bereaved families and the suffering of the whole of Northern Ireland would cease.

One of the obvious and crucial ways of beginning and consolidating a new way of thinking about the nature of a permanently peaceful society, which would have tolerance and respect for all, was to start with the young people. Gordon often said that his generation, and those before him, had failed the young, and it was up to the new generation to work for a better society. A number of the projects which were started as a result of the Enniskillen bomb had these priorities in mind, including the Marie Wilson Voyage For Hope.

Soon after the Enniskillen bomb in 1987, the then Canadian High Commissioner in London, His Excellency Roy McMurty, was so moved by Gordon's words on radio and television and by the suffering of all the families of the bereaved and injured that he decided to do something tangible in memory of those who had lost their lives. (In fact, he had been staying at Hillsborough Castle, near Belfast, with the then Secretary of State for Northern Ireland, Mr Tom King, when news of the Enniskillen bomb first broke, and his physical presence in Northern Ireland on that grim day may have added a deeper dimension to his personal commitment.)

He persuaded the Canadian Government to assist, and as a result he helped to set up the Marie Wilson Voyage for Hope. Since 1988, at least six young people have been selected each year to travel to Canada for a three-week visit in the summer. From the beginning, equal numbers of Protestants and Roman Catholics, and boys and girls, have been selected, and it was decided – a few years after the scheme started – to invite all post-primary schools in County Fermanagh to participate, rather than simply those from Enniskillen itself.

The three-week stay in Canada includes a period of several days with a host family in Toronto, and the rest of the time is spent in Moorelands Camp. This is based on an island which is over two hours' drive from Toronto, and it was set up for the benefit of socially deprived children from the city. The young people from Fermanagh act as leaders or counsellors during their stay at the camp. One of the central objectives is to build personal relationships with people from different religious backgrounds and cultures, and the young people who take part in the scheme are encouraged to maintain their friendships and contacts when they return home.

The scheme has been well supported by successive Canadian High Commissioners – including Roy McMurty, Donald McDonald, Fredrik Eaton and Royce Frith and their senior officials – and there has been important financial support from the International Fund for Ireland and Air Canada. The hosts in Canada have been extremely supportive, including the Macanuels and the Kellett families have taken part since the beginning, as well as John Latimer, the former Principal of St George's College and Marc Cote, the camp organizer.

Gordon and Joan always took a keen interest in the scheme, and one year Gordon himself was a member of the selection panel, so that he could have a first-hand opportunity to talk to the young people and to ask them why they wished to take part in the Voyage for Hope. Prior to the departure of the group each year, every successful applicant was given a copy of *Marie*, and on their return he faithfully attended the illustrated talks about their experiences. Jack Walls, the administrator of the scheme from the beginning, believes that the Marie Wilson Voyage for Hope has been one of the outstanding initiatives for peace and reconciliation in the Fermanagh area. A total of 56 young people have travelled to Canada in the first eight years, and they have shown great qualities of tolerance and a desire to live in friendship.

The 'Spirit of Enniskillen Bursaries' were established on the initiative of Ulsterman Dr Brian Mawhinney, who in 1987 was the Government minister in charge of education in Northern Ireland. Ten days after the bomb, he went personally to see Gordon at his home in Cooper Crescent, and some time later they met at Stormont, near Belfast, where Brian Mawhinney outlined his project. The idea was to encourage young people aged between sixteen and nineteen from Northern Ireland to travel outside the Province and to use their experience to help build community bridges at home.

The Bursaries are meant to expose young Ulster people to areas overseas where others are trying to cope with complex community problems, and to bring that experience back to Northern Ireland. The Government originally provided £150,000, and later increased the investment to £180,000. Also the American Ireland Fund (which was established by, among others, Dr Tony O'Reilly, Chairman and Chief Executive of the Heinz Corporation) helped by underwriting extra Bursaries. Since its inception, more than 300 young people have taken part in the scheme.

The flavour and the range of the visits was established right from the start, and the four original projects were all demanding and challenging. They included a study of the Navajo and Hopi Indians on a reservation in Arizona; an observation of the French-speaking and English-speaking Canadians in Quebec, where sadly, the divisions are not unlike some of those in Northern Ireland; a study of Northern Ireland expatriates in Boston; and the living and working conditions in an orphanage in Mexico.

The reactions of those young Northern Ireland people who visited such projects was informative and encouraging. One wrote: 'The whole experience in Mexico opened my eyes to the real world...the "Spirit of Enniskillen" showed me that the people of Northern Ireland are fighting over nothing. We are so insular and narrow-minded that we can't see we have no justification for war, no cause for fighting and definitely no right to judge who has the right to live.' Another young person wrote simply and tellingly: 'In a sense, the end of our travelling was merely the beginning.'

There were other positive developments that arose out of the horror of Enniskillen, including the establishment of Enniskillen Together, which encouraged outreach in local areas where there was a need for bridge-building. This was largely the idea of John Maxwell, whose son Paul was killed several years earlier by an IRA explosion which also killed Lord Mountbatten and members of his family, during a fishing trip at Mullaghmore in County Sligo. One of the successful projects was the establishment of an integrated school, where Protestant and Roman Catholic children are educated together. Some three weeks after the Enniskillen bomb, about 500 Fermanagh teachers from Protestant and Roman Catholic schools met in Enniskillen to discuss how mutual understanding, tolerance and reconciliation could be encouraged.

All these, and other, developments warmed Gordon's heart. He could see tangible results of bridge-building in his home county, after all he had been through. He knew, of course, that many people, including some of his Protestant acquaintances, disapproved. But such disapproval, and in some cases outright criticism, did not put him off. It particularly encouraged him that this was taking place among the young, as he believed passionately that they held the key to the future.

Gordon felt that quiet, sustained efforts at bridge-building were bound to pay dividends, not only in Enniskillen but in Northern Ireland as a whole. He sensed that while people were still holding on to their own ways of worshipping and looking at things, some blurring of the hard edges was indeed taking place. He said: 'I don't think Enniskillen will ever forget the bomb, but somehow it has made all of us realize that the old ways were not necessarily the best ways and that we have to keep working and hoping and co-operating for a better future.' He was once asked to define the 'Spirit of Enniskillen', and he replied: 'It is a spirit of love where there might have been hatred, of tolerance where there might have been retribution, and of reconciliation where there might have been division. With God's help, the "Spirit of Enniskillen" will point the way to a better future for everyone. Love can, and will, triumph over hatred.'

Gordon was anxious to share his experience with others who were living through the trauma of bereavement, and he identified closely with those who went through unspeakable suffering as a result of the IRA explosion at Warrington. On Saturday 20 March 1993 – the eve of Mother's Day – two IRA bombs exploded in a litter-bin at Bridge Street, killing Johnathan Ball, aged four, and very seriously injuring Tim Parry, who was twelve. Fifty-six other people were hurt, some of them badly. Tim Parry put up a heroic fight for life, but despite the best medical help available and the dedication of doctors and nurses, his injuries proved so extensive that the harrowing decision was taken five days later to switch off his life-support machine.

His parents, Colin and Wendy Parry, vividly described the agony of losing their son in their moving and thought-provoking book, *Tim – An Ordinary Boy*, and they told how Gordon came to sympathize with them on the day after Tim died. He had gone to Warrington to attend the funeral of Johnathan Ball. Colin himself could recall hearing Gordon's radio broadcast on the morning after Marie died, and his description of her last words – 'Daddy, I love you very much' – had reduced him to tears as he drove to work. He could not comprehend how any man could show such immense dignity in the face of such loss, and he had no inkling that he and Wendy would have to face the same heartbreak several years later. In the midst of their bereavement they, too, showed tremendous dignity and strength of character.

After the Warrington bomb a spontaneous wave of revulsion had swept through the Republic, and the work of Peace '93, which was formed by a Dublin woman named Susan McHugh, led to a number of massive street demonstrations in Dublin and elsewhere. The IRA were now becoming increasingly isolated. Their insistence that adequate warnings had been given was described by the police as a cynical ploy to divert blame. The general feeling of revulsion was exemplified by one of the many messages which were left at the scene of the blast. From 'A Warrington Couple', it said, 'May God forgive them, because we can't.'

Many messages of sympathy had come from Ireland, North and South, and Colin Parry, in the midst of his grief, told the media, 'We don't hold the Irish nation responsible. There is good and bad in every nation.' The Irish Deputy Prime Minister and Foreign Minister, Dick Spring, said in a message to the Warrington parents: 'It was not the real Ireland which plunged you into this nightmare. The real Ireland is walking in spirit behind the coffins of your sons.' The *Belfast Telegraph* perceptively headlined its editorial on Warrington 'England's Enniskillen?', and in many ways it was. There was the same sense of shock over the death of innocent children, and the agonized reaction of the parents all over again.

Long before the Warrington bomb, Gordon often said that it was only those with experience of a similar bereavement who could understand what such a devastating loss really meant. So when Gordon visited Colin and Wendy Parry on the morning after Tim died, he knew instinctively the depth of their suffering. He knew also what it meant to have to suffer so grievously in the full light of publicity, and how little real privacy the family would be given at a time when they needed all their inner resources to come to terms with the loss of their son.

Colin and Wendy recount in their book how Gordon spoke with conviction and compassion and, above all, with great emotion. He told them that even though it was more than five years since Marie's death, he still cried openly for the loss which he and Joan had suffered. Significantly, he also told them that Tim's death would place a strain on family relationships and that they should realize that, although they were married, they would not necessarily grieve in the same way, or at the same time. Gordon was speaking directly from his own and Joan's experience. He said that resentment could easily occur at times of deep grieving and that they must find ways of venting these feelings and differences, which would otherwise become destructive. It was sound advice and was helpful in the agonizing months ahead. They said, 'We knew that we had been in the company of a good man.' Gordon also spent time with Wilf and Marie Ball, the parents of Johnathan, and with John Donlan, who later became co-ordinator of the Warrington Project. He simply sat and listened to their grief, and said that in time to come people would turn to them in times of tragedy, knowing that their grief would be understood.

That visit began a firm friendship between the Wilsons and the Parrys. Gordon was unable to attend Tim's funeral, but he made a point of being present at the launch of the Warrington Project in October 1993. It was initiated by civic and political leaders in the town, and one of its main aims is to enable people from Warrington, Northern Ireland and the Irish Republic to spend time in each other's communities and to help to create friendship and better understanding of each other's cultures.

Such a project was close to Gordon's heart, and he spoke at a weekend seminar connected with its launch. In his speech he confirmed that prior to the Warrington bombs on 20 March, he had planned to announce through the *Sunday Times* and other media his public challenge to the leadership of the IRA. He also talked about his meeting with them: 'I can tell you that I talked about Warrington when I spoke to the IRA because they assured me that they were carrying on a war against the security forces, the police and the army. And I said to them, "How can you explain that in Warrington you let off two bombs and you killed two little children?" I don't understand the word "sorry".

They were sorry. It was the only time I raised my voice in my talk with them, but they were unmoved. It proved to me how entrenched they are.'

Colin and Gordon shared a platform on several occasions. Together they bore witness to the harsh reality that suffering knows no boundaries. The Warrington Project continues to attract wide support in Northern Ireland, and the excellent and award-winning Warrington Male Voice Choir, a staunch and collective supporter of the Project, regularly visits the Province, where it is invariably received with warmth and appreciation.

Colin and Wendy, and two other representatives from Warrington, attended Gordon's funeral service, where they were seated in the Wilsons' family pew. Joan still retains a great regard and respect for her friends in Warrington, including John Donlan, the brother-in-law of Wilf Ball. She was particularly touched to receive a card and a candle from the Warrington Project on the first Easter after Gordon's death. To her it symbolized that the 'Spirit of Enniskillen' and the 'Spirit of Warrington' are one. John Donlan, a caring man, speaks highly of Joan and the affection with which she is regarded in Warrington.

Seven months after the Warrington tragedy, an IRA bomb exploded without warning on Belfast's Shankill Road at a busy Saturday lunchtime. Ten people were killed, including the niece of a man who was a member of a Belfast Salvation Army Band which had been invited to play in Warrington. John Donlon says: 'As Gordon foretold, this man sought me out and told me in great detail of the events of that terrible day, and how he had searched through the rubble with his bare hands to recover the remains of his niece. All I could do was hold his hand and listen.'

After the bombing in their town, the people of Warrington made the site of the explosion in Bridge Street into a 'shrine' by laying a carpet of flowers. The children brought their soft toys, mainly teddy bears. Flowers and toys by the plane-load arrived from Ireland. The toys were collected, and most of them were donated to local playgroups and to children with special needs. Some went to children living on the so-called Peace Line in Belfast. John Donlan says: 'We felt that a special gesture was due to the people of Ireland, who had written to us in great numbers and who had unanimously and unequivocally dissociated themselves from the men of violence. Gordon very kindly agreed to take one of the bears back to Dublin and present it, on our behalf, to President Robinson. We sent the bear "In memory of a little boy who never lost his innocence". The President accepted the bear on behalf of the people of Ireland.'

Gordon and the President had met several times previously and had become friends. President Robinson recalls the day of the Enniskillen explosion and being totally devastated, like so many others. She had friends in Enniskillen, and as a Senator she had stayed in Portora Royal School, where she knew one of the teachers. 'The explosion was profoundly shocking and depressing, and more so than many other outrages because of the scale of the deaths and suffering which had taken place in the lovely old town of Enniskillen.'

Some time afterwards she met Gordon at a peace meeting in Dublin. 'What struck me then, and remained with me since and became more pronounced, was the fact that he reminded me of my father, though he was much younger. They had the same incredible personal integrity.'

When Mary Robinson was elected President of Ireland she invited Gordon as one of her personal guests to her Inauguration, both as a symbol and also as a friend. 'He symbolized the reconciliation which can come out of suffering, and the capacity to bring good out of evil. This requires a particular quality, a particular generosity, and a particular strength of spirit and of spirituality.'

Their close relationship continued, and she used to tease him about his smoking. 'When I became President he began to call me "President Mary", and I said, "Don't let this come between us." He replied, "Of course not, President Mary!" That was him. I was "The President" to him, and we went into a different phase. As President I saw more of him in valuable ways than previously, but essentially our relationship did not change. It was warm. We embraced when we met, which is not necessarily the relationship I have with many other people. We were very close.'

As President, Mary Robinson visited Enniskillen, at Gordon's request, to talk to the Rotary Club and to carry out a number of other engagements. She had a private meeting with most of the relatives of those who had been in the Enniskillen explosion. She was particularly concerned by the way in which all the relatives were still so deeply affected, many years later.

When Gordon died she felt a deep, personal loss. His legacy, she believes, will endure not only because of his immediate response in showing generosity, courage and reconciliation, but because of the fact that he sustained this response, and lived it out. 'In the aftermath of the Enniskillen bombing he helped a lot of us to cope with the grief. Somehow he made it possible to accept that this awful thing had happened, but that it was possible for something positive to come out of it, because he was saying so. He was such a special person. His death was a personal loss to me, remarkably so.'

The President attended the launch of the Warrington Project, as did Prince Charles. In her speech, she said that ordinary people in Belfast, Dublin and Warrington had begun to put into words and actions the revulsion and sense of injustice they rightly felt at the taking of lives for political ends – whether Irish or British, Nationalist or Unionist, Catholic or Protestant. She said it was clear that at community level in Britain and Ireland there was a strong awareness of the futility and injustice of violence, and a burning desire for peace.

Though there were many messages of sympathy and peace demonstrations in Northern Ireland after the Warrington deaths, there was also an air of bewilderment that there had been such an upsurge of revulsion in England and in the Irish Republic. Some Ulster people, while grieving for those bereaved and injured in Warrington, were very conscious that the blood-drip had gone on and on in Northern Ireland and that most people outside the Province had seemed to pay very little attention.

President Robinson mentioned this in her speech at the launch of the Warrington Project. She said that there were places in Northern Ireland where the death of children and the destruction of homes and families were such a regular occurrence that they no longer attracted major attention or outrage. There were many individuals who, as well as having to bear the suffering of violence, had also to endure the indifference that routine violence attracts. She added: 'In all humility, the spirit of Warrington should pay tribute to their endurance, should include their suffering, and understand their pain.'

One of the remarkable aspects of the Gordon Wilson story is the degree to which he attracted sympathy and support from outside Northern Ireland. That is not to say that he did not attract enormous good-will and admiration within the Province as well. He had his critics in Ulster, some of them stern and unforgiving, but he had very many supporters as well. But his acceptance in the Irish Republic was particularly widespread. It was almost as if people there, who had largely escaped the kind of violence that had plagued the North (though there were a number of deaths and horrific incidents in the Republic as well) had found a Northerner who had helped them to open the flood-gates of their sympathy for the victims and to express their disgust at the violence, in a way that they had not quite been able to do before, or to such a degree.

From the start Gordon had been in a position to convey that the very symbolism of the Poppy and of Remembrance Day itself had been attacked by the bomb. Dr John Robb, who as a former Senator himself, knew well the Southern psyche. He believes that there was a feeling of guilt in the South about not having been so affected by the cruelty and violence in the North. 'By taking Gordon Wilson into their feelings, they were able to handle their own sense of guilt a bit better.' John Dardis, a Southerner and a close colleague of Gordon in the Senate, recognized the degree to which he struck up a rapport with the people of the Republic and they with him. He says, 'They saw in Gordon something they could identify with, something that they themselves wished they could be. They saw in him an ability to show such Christianity in such terrible circumstances, and yet he was also a very approachable human being. Maybe we all realized he was something which we all wished we could be.'

In April 1996, Joan attended a memorial service for Gordon at Clongowes Wood College, near Dublin, where the special preacher was his Church of Ireland friend Dean John McCarthy. It was a most uplifting experience. The Reverend Bruce Bradley SJ, Principal of the College, said later that Gordon's response to the tragedy of Enniskillen, his 'magnanimity' in accepting a seat on the Irish Senate, his work for the Forum, and his overwhelming goodness and palpable sincerity spoke volumes to the people of the South. 'For most people down here, whether he was Catholic or Protestant was not important. I can only try to imagine that Northern Protestants were tempted to see him as too accommodating, too forgiving, almost – and in the minds of some, no doubt – actually to the point of betrayal.'

Gordon knew and understood this only too well, yet he had a sense of vision which transcended his personal trauma, and, borne on a tide of popular feeling that the violence must stop, he found the courage to face up to an inner challenge that had been gnawing at him since Marie had died. A backbone of steel in this man of sensitivity and forgiveness was clearly seen in his decision, publicized on the day after the Warrington bombs, to challenge the Provisional IRA leadership to a face-to-face confrontation.

12

In the Lions' Den

On Sunday 21 March 1993 the *Sunday Times* and other news media carried details of Gordon's carefully prepared statement to the IRA. He acknowledged that no community had a monopoly of suffering or grief, that no side was entirely to blame for what had occurred, and that all were guilty and were also victims. He noted, however, that common guilt and suffering should not lead to paralysis, moral ambivalence or fatalism. He underlined that everyone needed to stand up for that they believed in, but at the same time to be able to distinguish right from wrong. And his words to those who killed Marie were blunt and uncompromising:

> When I expressed my forgiveness for my daughter Marie's killers, I did not mean to excuse what you had done. The explanations you offered were unconvincing, and in any case, there can never be an acceptable explanation for placing high explosives near fragile human flesh. I must tell you frankly that when a bomb is placed in a town centre and people are killed as a result, there is no mistake and no excuse. What I meant to do in expressing forgiveness was to set aside personal vengeance and bitterness, which in turn denied the Loyalist paramilitaries any grounds for using my bereavement as a pretext for imposing suffering on Nationalists, Catholics, Republicans or IRA members. I wanted no revenge, no bitterness and no grief for other families.
>
> I did not mean, in extending Christian forgiveness to your comrades who planned, caused and then excused my daughter's death, to imply that their actions were in any way justifiable, reasoned or understandable. They were not. The actions of paramilitaries on

all sides are abhorrent to me and to the majority of the rest of the people on this island.

He stressed, however, that he shared a common humanity with those who carried out the 'massacre' and with other 'Republicans'. He said:

> Many of you have been bereaved as I have been, and many of you have suffered as much or more than I have. All of you must hope that your children will live free of suffering and fear and that the future will be better for them than the past has been for our generation. It is on this common ground of shared experience and hope that we can meet.

Gordon knew that by this gesture he would attract severe criticism from those who believed that he was naive and that by talking to the IRA he would give them the oxygen of publicity they so craved. He also knew that there was little likelihood that they would immediately announce an end to their violence, but he felt that as Marie Wilson's father he had a unique moral claim to be taken seriously by them. He expected, at the very least, an indication of a shift in their hitherto uncompromising stand, and perhaps an assurance that an internal debate was taking place which might lead in the end to a fundamental reappraisal of their policy of using violence for political ends.

There was no immediate reply from the IRA, nor did Gordon expect one. His statement had been comprehensive in its outline of shared guilt, common suffering, and moral condemnation of all killing, including the death of his daughter Marie. The challenge was pitched in such a way that the IRA could not ignore it outright, and certainly not without some credible attempt at an explanation for doing so. Gordon was confident that there would be a response, but he was by no means clear as to what that response might be. In the meantime he waited with a mixture of nervousness and anticipation, but he was convinced that he was doing the right thing. Some three days later, the IRA issued a statement in Dublin confirming that it would meet Gordon Wilson and that a 'representative' would be in touch with him in due course.

Joan and Gordon had discussed a possible meeting with the IRA some time after Marie died. They had asked themselves many times how anyone could have inflicted the death and injuries of Enniskillen on innocent civilians. They had both expressed a desire to confront those who had killed Marie to ask them, 'Why did you do this? What purpose has it achieved? Have you any idea of the suffering you have caused to so many people? Do you even care about such grief? What will you say to God on your day of judgement when you are asked to account for your actions?' These questions lay deep in Gordon's mind for several years, until he threw down the gauntlet to the IRA. Joan says: 'From the very start I encouraged him to meet the IRA. If he hadn't been prepared to consider it, I would have gone myself. We talked about it a great deal, and Gordon took it all on board. For a long, long time he mulled it over, and then suddenly he moved. That was often his way of doing things.'

Gordon's critics responded much sooner than the IRA. Some of the relatives of the other victims of Enniskillen were particularly outspoken. Aileen Quinton, whose mother died in the blast, was described by the *Sunday Life* newspaper in Belfast as being 'deeply saddened' by Gordon's plan. She said, 'I strongly believe that it will do more harm than good, by giving encouragement and validity to the IRA's cause.'

James Mullan, who lost both parents in the Enniskillen blast, said Gordon Wilson did not speak for him or his family. Stella Robinson told the newspaper that she did not want the memories of her parents, who also died at Enniskillen, to be 'sullied' by meetings with terrorists. Yet another Enniskillen man whose father died at the Cenotaph commented anonymously that Gordon Wilson must realize the hostility to what he proposed to do: 'He should take that into account before making these grandiose gestures', he said.

Gordon, in answer to the condemnation, said that he understood the relatives' point of view and that they had a perfect right to state how they felt. He had never forgotten the others who had suffered as a result of the Enniskillen bomb, but he had never claimed to represent their point of view. From the very start he had spoken for himself as Marie Wilson's dad.

Gordon was a sensitive man and he felt deeply the criticisms of those who had suffered as he had done. A relative of one of the Enniskillen victims said that forgiveness and compassion for the bombers had been forced down their throats, whether they agreed with it or not. 'It got to the stage where we were made to feel that there was something wrong with us because we were not falling over ourselves to forgive the IRA unconditionally.'

Such views are understandable in the context of such a horrific experience as the Enniskillen bombing. People have their own ways of trying to cope with trauma and tragedy. It is worth recording, however, that there were those who also echoed Gordon's words of forgiveness. The Reverend Robert Armstrong, a Methodist minister, spoke at the funeral service of his brother Wesley and sister-in-law Bertha who died in the explosion. In the summer of 1995 he wrote an article in *Christian Healing* (the magazine of the Churches' Council for Health and Healing in Ireland) and reflected on his feelings at the time of the explosion and on the need for forgiveness. He wrote:

Denying Christ's forgiveness to others means His healing cannot flow into us and through us to others. Some one has said 'I love God only as much as I love my worst enemy.'

But Gordon also received support from others for his plan. He had taken soundings from colleagues and associates whose political judgement he respected, including Albert Reynolds, who later played a leading role in brokering the IRA ceasefire which was announced on 31 August 1994. Reynolds recalls: 'I did not discourage Gordon in seeking such a meeting but counselled him not to be disappointed at the outcome.'

When Gordon issued his challenge, he suggested that Mitchell McLaughlin, a Sinn Fein councillor from Londonderry, or a member of the National Graves Association in Dublin, should help him to make contact with the IRA. McLaughlin, not surprisingly, declined to act as a go-between. Sinn Fein members continually denied any connection between the two organizations, despite widespread disbelief among the media and the general public. Nevertheless, moves were being made behind the scenes. After the IRA had publicly announced that they would meet him, it was only a question of time and of location.

Four days after his initial challenge to the IRA, Gordon returned to his theme during his maiden speech at the Irish Senate. Not surprisingly, this had a wide audience, as he had been making headline news for most of that week. He repeated his challenge to the IRA in clear but statesmanlike language, and he asked for the support of Senate members in his intentions, even if they would find it difficult for party political reasons to engage the IRA in dialogue themselves.

In early April he received the news he had been waiting for. The clandestine groundwork had paid off, and the IRA indicated privately through an intermediary that they were willing to meet him within days at a destination unspecified. The first that Joan heard of the actual meeting itself was during a brief and tense phone call from Gordon on the morning of 7 April while she was at Gortatole Community Centre, near Enniskillen, where she was rehearsing for a concert that evening. Gordon said: 'Things are moving. I have been told not to bring my own vehicle, so I will need your car. Try not to worry about me – I'll be all right. I'll phone you later on, when it's all over.' Then he hung up.

Joan felt her heart pounding. She had expected this to happen, but when the news came it was nonetheless disturbing, even frightening. She knew that it stood to reason that Gordon would not be harmed. Even the IRA were shrewd enough to imagine the enormous public outcry which would result on all sides if they laid a finger on Gordon Wilson. But these were the people who had killed her daughter, and she knew that Gordon was going into the lions' den. She prayed for his safety, but she could not share her fears with her companions. The meeting was totally secret, and any breach of family security could mean that it would be called off. Both Julie Anne and Peter had been told in confidence, and both were extremely concerned for their father's safety. A long, anxious day lay ahead for the whole family.

Though Joan knew in advance that such a meeting would take place, Gordon never shared any of the planning details with her. He took the view that the fewer people who knew, the better. Anyhow, his ability for remaining tight-lipped was well known to his family. Some years earlier, when Julie Anne and John had decided to become engaged, John formally asked Gordon for his daughter's hand in marriage. Gordon naturally agreed, and also promised, at their request, not to tell anyone else, including Joan, until it was formally announced by the couple at Christmas as a 'surprise'. A man who would not tell his own wife about their daughter's engagement was hardly likely to tell her in advance any details about meeting the IRA.

From comments he made afterwards, however, Joan and the other family members were able to piece together some details. At the IRA's request, Gordon drove to Donegal town in Joan's car and not his own, and left the vehicle in a car-park. He was then taken by two drivers on a series of twisting roads, so that he became totally disorientated. Joan believes that a Donegal member of Sinn Fein, and also a Protestant minister, were involved in part of this process. The car journey ended at a bungalow, and Gordon was taken in to a front room. He was received courteously by two people – a man wearing a cap and glasses and a young woman. Neither was masked. They offered him tea and pastries.

At the start of the meeting, they handed him a typed statement, which they released afterwards to the media. It was entitled 'To Senator Gordon Wilson from the leadership of the IRA'. Gordon said later that he found this strange, as if they had already made up their minds before they talked to him. Some people believed that this was an act of extreme cynicism on their part, and implied that whatever Gordon said, the IRA members were in no mood to change their minds.

The IRA statement began by offering personally their sincere 'condolences and apologies' for the death of Marie, who, 'along with other innocent civilians, died as a result of one of our operations'. They welcomed the fact that Gordon had publicly acknowledged that they in the Republican community had also suffered losses and had had to bear grief 'in equal measure'. They also welcomed the fact that Gordon, in spite of his loss, had had the courage to point out that all who had suffered had an equal and vested interest in establishing peace, including the Republican movement.

However, they continued in the kind of stereotyped language that is familiar to those who have studied Republican statements: 'It is our view that peace will only come about as a result of a process which takes as its starting point the proven failure of partition and which accepts the fundamental right of the Irish people to self-determination.' They called for inclusive dialogue, without preconditions, in a spirit of generosity and with leadership and courage. They added: 'For our part, we in the IRA will not be found wanting in this regard.' They ended with familiar Republican rhetoric: 'The root cause of this conflict is the historic and ongoing violent denial of Irish national rights.'

For Gordon, sitting in the room and holding a copy of *Marie* for comfort and strength, it was not a promising start. It appeared from their statement that the IRA were not prepared to budge an inch from their traditional demand for a British withdrawal from Northern Ireland, and there was no indication of any fundamental rethink on their part about the use of violence. But Gordon, having come this far, bravely battled on. He talked about the suffering as a result of the bombs in Enniskillen and Warrington, and other atrocities. The IRA listened but were unmoved.

He later revealed more details of the meeting to the media and to his family and some close friends, but in searching through his papers I found a typed summary of the proceedings which seems to have been supplied to him afterwards by the IRA. Joan had no knowledge of this, and Gordon had never mentioned it to her. There are a number of important gaps, as if the note-taker had insufficiently fast shorthand, or could not make out the details of a tape-recording, but it does give a flavour of the discussion.

Significantly, the document refers to a 'Meeting between GW and 3 reps of IRA'. Gordon never referred to a third person, who presumably was the note-taker but who also played a role in the discussions. The conversation begins with a preamble from Gordon, seeking assurances that the people he is speaking to are representatives of the IRA leadership and not 'messengers'. The document does not record whether or not he did receive any assurances on this.

An IRA spokesman gives the reasons for taking notes of the meeting: 'It's our experience that the media can and have lifted specific sections of reported meetings. The record we have of the meeting allows us to have an accurate record from which we can quote.'

Gordon also welcomes a record of the proceedings, and then launches into a long explanation of why he had sought a face-to-face encounter. He tells the IRA: 'I think you accept my motives are honest and pure. I've given a lot of thought and a lot of prayer to this meeting.' This first section seems a little disjointed, either because of the poor note-taking or because of Gordon's nervousness. He talks about Marie's death, about forgiveness, and also about the pressure he feels from those who criticized him for seeking such a meeting. 'The next death in Enniskillen or Fermanagh or Northern Ireland, they'll say, "That's what came of him meeting the IRA."'

An IRA voice interrupts to talk about the 'root cause', as if they want to get down to politics. But Gordon is not put off his stride: 'I asked to see the IRA, not Sinn Fein or the UDA, because it was the IRA who killed my daughter. I'm not here as a politician. I lay for two years asking, "What can I do to bring peace?" The answer that came up was to go and see the people who killed Marie. Go as her father. It's only in the last six months that I've got up the strength. I've lost friends over this. "Go and play golf," they say, but it's in here [indicates heart]. Others have talked to Sinn Fein, others to the UDA, but nobody to the IRA.' (Strictly speaking, Gordon was wrong about this, as a number of Protestant clergymen and others met the IRA leadership in the Irish Republic some years previously, but one can understand his lack of fine detail on such an occasion.)

Gordon then declares that if the IRA would abandon the armed struggle, 'and I don't mean a ceasefire', the Loyalists would respond, though not necessarily the next day. He tells the IRA that their organization and Sinn Fein will never be able to get round a table for negotiations, without abandoning the campaign of violence.

One of the IRA members replies: 'First of all, we can see that you are sincere, but it is naive to think that the IRA hold the key to peace. Republicans want peace.' Reference is made to the 1920s, 1930s and 1940s (presumably meaning previous and abortive IRA campaigns), and to the formation of the Civil Rights Movement in 1969. This is followed by several short exchanges, which read as follows:

> GW: I've said my piece. I don't want to get into an argumentative situation.
>
> IRA: We listened to you without agreeing or interrupting.
>
> GW: My silence doesn't mean that I agree with what you say.
>
> IRA: You've lost Marie, a young woman with her life in front of her. The Republican community have suffered also and want peace.
>
> Note-taker: I took notes so as not to break your train of thought. There are two levels on which we must examine things – it's personal and it's on the level of politics and social (sic) and economics. I know what loss is like.
>
> GW: On that level we share a common humanity.
>
> IRA: We all share a common humanity, no matter who we are.

Gordon then talks about reconciliation with God, and quotes John 3. He emphasizes that the IRA are not totally to blame for loss of life, though they killed his daughter. He says he has doubts about what they really want – does wanting the 'Brits' out mean that they want Protestants out as well?

An IRA speaker replies, 'Definitely not.' There is then a reference to 'Loyalist deaths squads' and to the Enniskillen bomb. 'The IRA made a statement pointing out...we are fighting a war, and in a war situation things go wrong. Bloody Sunday. It was not our intention to kill Protestants. If it were our intention, they could be killed in their tens. Look at Iraq.'

An IRA speaker then launches into a condemnation of the partition of Ireland and points out that the Loyalists threatened force against the creation of an independent, united Ireland (in the early part of the century), and describes Northern Ireland as 'an artificially created state'.

Gordon begins to sound exasperated and exclaims, 'I've heard it all a thousand times!'

He listens to the other speaker claim that 'It is the force of the IRA which brought the question of change on to the agenda' and that it is the IRA's ultimate aim that everybody can live 'on this island free from British interference'.

Gordon retorts sharply, 'You're blaming the Brits. You're saying it's because of the British that Marie is dead. You're walking into the lions' den. I didn't expect to be brought here and shown the door or be given a direct response of ending the armed struggle, but I did expect some indication that would show a response. Give me some joy.'

The exchanges continue in the same tone, and they reach an impasse. Gordon says, with almost a note of despair, 'You have said nothing new to me, I have detected no change. We've talked, I've listened, you have listened, I can't say any more than this. I'm a little disappointed. I wanted some sense of a shift in the thinking of the IRA. I have not sensed such a shift. What can I say to the press?'

The IRA replies, 'The initiative lies with the British.'

Gordon ends by saying, 'I've heard it all before. I had it all to gain, my heart has been eased. I'll sleep contentedly. I've done what I had not the guts to do for two years.'

At this point the meeting starts to break up and the note-taking or tape-recording ceases. The document ends with the following words: 'These notes are being forwarded to you as requested. As you are aware, the IRA have a copy of the notes also, which at this stage will not be published in any shape, manner or form. Your decision regarding the future of these notes is entirely up to you, but the IRA will not get involved in any public discussions regarding the contents.'

Unfortunately, these notes are an imperfect record of the discussions, but they do confirm Gordon's later assessment to the media that there was absolutely no meeting of minds. The tone of the exchanges and especially Gordon's replies after his first lengthy statement also indicate that he became more and more dispirited as the talks continued. Even before he reached the end, it is clear that he felt that he had been naive and that he was wasting his time.

He was driven back to Donegal town, where he phoned Joan around 8.30 p.m., and he arrived home about two hours later. He was weary and emotional as he shared a cup of tea with his family. Julie Anne recalls: 'He was in a terrible state. He was totally shocked by the IRA's response, and he kept saying over and over, "There's no hope for this country."' He felt that they would continue their campaign of violence for ten, twenty, thirty years, indeed for as long as it took to remove the British presence in Northern Ireland. He was shaken to the core by their tunnel vision and by the lack of even a glimmer of a rethink about their fundamental strategy. Joan says: 'He could not get over the fact that they were so determined and articulate, and hard. He could get nothing at all out of the man in the cap, but he felt that there was a certain acknowledgement of him in personal terms from the girl. He thought she might be a graduate, and as he looked at her he thought of Marie.'

Gordon and Joan had a sleepless night because of the high emotion of the previous day and the disappointing outcome. The next morning Gordon fended off television interviews at his home and left early for Belfast, where he gave a press conference. When Joan saw him later on television she was shocked at how worn and weary he looked. At the press conference Gordon, in typical fashion, pulled no punches. At times he seemed near to tears, and he admitted with characteristic candour that his meeting had been pointless. He had hoped to persuade the IRA to lay down their arms, but said, 'Perhaps it was naive of me to imagine that because it was me, they would. The bottom line for me was peace, but I got nothing, and in that sense, perhaps I was duped.'

Predictably, Unionist politicians heaped criticism on him. Sammy Wilson, the outspoken Press Officer for the Democratic Unionists, said that Gordon had given the IRA a huge propaganda weapon and that he 'should be hanging his head in shame'. He was also attacked by some political commentators, including Geoffrey Wheatcroft of the *Daily Mail*, who wrote that Gordon Wilson had met 'evil people'. In so doing, Wheatcroft declared, he had undermined his own decency and goodness, and he had undermined all who must learn that sometimes evil must be fought with force. Gordon was also criticized for meeting the IRA on the same day as a memorial service was being held for the victims of the Warrington bomb. His critics believed that the timing of the meeting had been an IRA tactic to divert attention from the Warrington service, but Gordon had been given no choice in the matter.

A number of people supported Gordon publicly, including the then Labour Party spokesman on Northern Ireland, Kevin McNamara, who said, 'I share Mr Wilson's disappointment but I congratulate him on his efforts.' Peter Temple-Morris, the Tory co-chairman of the British-Irish Inter-Parliamentary Body, said, 'I admire the noble gesture of a noble man.' John Hume, leader of the Social Democratic and Labour Party, praised Gordon's courage and said, 'He showed himself to be a man of deep, deep Christian charity and tolerance in what he did.' The Reverend Nigel Baylor, a Church of Ireland minister from Newtownbutler, wrote to the local paper, *The Impartial Reporter*, to defend Gordon. He stated: 'On the day when Gordon Wilson met with members of the IRA, there was only one side which was in the wrong. Let that be clearly stated.' He was also praised by an anonymous letter-writer in the *Belfast Telegraph* who referred to the Christianity which Gordon revealed at the news conference, and stated: 'He is so different from the so-called politicians who criticized him. Apart from John Hume, their arrogance and supercilious attitude was sickening.'

Despite such support, Gordon steeled himself for the torrent of criticism which he knew must come, and did come, and he felt anything but 'noble'. He was exhausted, and he felt that he had failed utterly. Joan knew more than anyone the intensity with which he had sought and had prepared for such a meeting. He had been thinking about it for years, and when it actually looked like happening, he had to summon all his depths of courage to meet the IRA face to face. He believed in his heart that they would listen to Gordon Wilson, if not to anyone else. He was shattered to realize that to them he was just another victim of violence and that they were prepared to kill many more people to get their way. He felt that he had met a brick wall and that nothing and nobody would shift the IRA. He became so disillusioned that shortly afterwards he called for the selective internment without trial of paramilitary leaders, including the IRA, on both sides of the border. He believed that if those people could not be persuaded to stop their violence, they would have to be taken out of circulation for the greater good of society. He still prayed for those who killed his daughter, but his forgiveness had acquired a hard, pragmatic edge. He told the media: 'If the gunmen won't go away, let's put them behind bars.'

Privately, however, he felt that in one way the meeting with the IRA had done him good. It had been a catharsis, after many months of waiting and worrying. Joan feels that he was more at peace with himself afterwards. She says: 'He believed that he had done all he could do. He had wanted to confront the IRA face to face, before he himself would meet his Maker. He did it for Marie, for the others and for me, and I think he also did it for himself.'

After this disturbing and deeply disappointing meeting with the IRA, he was at pains to remain on courteous terms with Sinn Fein, the political wing of the Republican movement. On the first day of the Forum he pointedly shook hands with Gerry Adams, the Sinn Fein President, though he was determined not to be used by anyone. He told me, for example, that he was extremely wary of allowing himself to be photographed with Adams. They did make personal contact, and they had a private meeting together. It was held at the request of Gerry Adams, and took place in a private room in Dublin Castle, which at that time was the venue for the meetings of the Forum for Peace and Reconciliation. Gordon told Joan very few details of the meeting, and he chose not to publicize it or to talk about it privately among friends and acquaintances, for fear of being misrepresented and attacked yet again by his critics.

Gerry Adams recalls that the meeting lasted about half an hour, and that it was not adversarial but was rather in the nature of a philosophic discussion. There was no point-scoring. 'I asked to see him because I thought it was important to meet in a circumstance which did not impinge on my sense of who I am or his sense of who he was. I wanted to express personally and on behalf of Sinn Fein my deep regret that his daughter had been killed, and also to see how we could help the situation along from each of our different perspectives.'

Adams was impressed by Gordon's sense of 'old-fashioned gentlemanliness' and his charm, which he used in his inimitably disarming way. But Adams recognized his undoubted sincerity. 'I would have made an effort in the circumstances to have talked to anyone who had been in his situation but I don't think that I would have been able to do so with the same sense of self-assurance, in that I knew he would not be jumping all over me and looking for a row. He was very gracious.'

Gordon talked about himself, about his family, about the inner conviction which told him that he should be slowing down a little, and the other inner, contradictory voices which told him that he should go on trying as best he could in a non-party-political way to improve the situation.

Though Gordon talked philosophically about a possible united Ireland, he did not advocate it, and Gerry Adams regarded him as a Unionist, perhaps with a small 'u'. He also looked on Gordon as a person with a special background – having been brought up in Leitrim and having lived his adult life in Fermanagh. He seemed, to Adams, to have a special sense of Irishness that stemmed from his cross-border experience. 'He had a very good sense of himself and he knew where he was at.'

On the day after the Enniskillen explosion, Gerry Adams had issued a short statement expressing the regret of the Republican movement at what had happened. Anything longer or more personal would have undoubtedly added to the immense anger of countless people and would have fuelled the fury of those who rightly blamed the IRA for their barbarity. In private he had his own views. 'It was devastating. What happened was totally wrong in itself, from its very conception. I was deeply moved by Gordon Wilson's account of the death of his daughter and deeply moved by his forgiveness.'

Such words, even today, will sound hollow to those who lost loved ones in the Enniskillen blast and in many other IRA killings. They will also be regarded by many others simply as a cynical public-relations exercise by a shrewd and tough political operator like Adams. They could also be the truth. Adams says: 'Universally there has to be view among Republicans that Gordon Wilson was a decent guy, that Enniskillen was a disaster, that it should not have happened to him or his family, that he dealt with it extremely well and that he showed great Christian forbearance. The feeling was that Gordon Wilson was a nice man and a very decent human being.'

That said, Adams believes that there is another element. 'At the back of the mind and the front of the mind of Republicans there is the question, "Why do we not have the same focus on those who were killed and maimed by the security forces and the Loyalist paramilitaries?"' This is not a question of "Whataboutery" or the politics of the latest atrocity. He says: 'It is part of the grieving process and the need for recognition of the suffering of all those who have lost relatives. When someone as able and as articulate as Gordon Wilson came through his horrific experience and received such publicity, it is understandable that others who had also suffered grievously began to ask why there was no such recognition of their suffering.'

This is precisely the point which was made about the other victims of the Enniskillen bombing, because those families were victims too. Ironically, the words of the Sinn Fein President could equally apply to the other Enniskillen victims, as well as all victims of violence, including Republicans. In the horrific and tragic story of Northern Ireland there is a dark symmetry of suffering on all sides.

Adams had not told his Sinn Fein colleagues about the meeting in advance, and he still regards it as a personal matter. His estimation of Gordon Wilson increased, and the meeting was important to him both as a human being and as an Irish Republican. 'I have met with the victims and the families of victims of the IRA, and it was important from my point of view to have that meeting with Gordon Wilson and to come away with my sense of Irish Republicanism intact, having had a conversation with a man who had been the victim of armed Republicanism.'

Gordon was quoted in one press report as saying that Gerry Adams had the kind of eyes that could not look at him straight. What he told a friend was, 'Gerry Adams has cold eyes, but I trust him. I have no other alternative.'

Having talked to Adams at some length myself, I was surprised not so much by Gordon's statement as by his hint of Adams' cold detachment. Gordon was always an astute judge of character. As Gordon may have done, I thought hard about such a meeting in case of misrepresentation, but my main guideline was, 'What would Gordon have done?' No doubt he would have talked to Gerry Adams in the same circumstances.

My own view is that Adams was indeed affected by the Enniskillen bombing and that he was personally impressed by Gordon's reaction.

Equally, he had a clear detachment in that he placed the Enniskillen horror in the context of all suffering, including that of the Republican movement. He also had the studied detachment of someone who has a long-term agenda and strategy, and who is determined that nothing and no one will allow him to be deflected from those objectives. This is perhaps the professional coldness which Gordon detected. But there is no doubt that the two men, from very different parts of the spectrum, had held a mutually significant meeting. They agreed to meet again if they thought such a meeting would achieve a further purpose, but no more such meetings took place before Gordon's sudden and unexpected death.

Gordon also told me privately that he had had an 'altercation' with Martin McGuinness, another Sinn Fein leader whom he regarded as a 'hard' man, at a closed session of the Forum. He said that McGuinness was making a speech demanding not just the reform, but the disbandment, of the Royal Ulster Constabulary, and accused them of numerous acts of wrongdoing against the Nationalist people. Gordon could stand this no longer and interrupted him to point out that he could not bear to hear, unchallenged, such accusations from a man whose associates had killed his daughter. There the exchange finished, but at the end of the debate McGuinness made a statement and apologized to Gordon, and said that his remarks had not been personal to the Wilson family. He promised that this would not happen again. Gordon appreciated the gesture and they shook hands. That story reveals something about Martin McGuinness and a great deal about the power of Gordon's very presence at the Forum. A seasoned observer at the Forum said that Sinn Fein in particular always listened very carefully when Gordon spoke. 'He was always "one up" on them because everybody knew that the IRA had killed his daughter.'

Some people claimed at the time that the Enniskillen bombing could prove to be a turning-point. Subsequent events in the intervening period would challenge that view, but as the years pass there is a sense that Enniskillen was indeed a watershed. David McKittrick, the Ireland correspondent of the London *Independent*, noted in Gordon's obituary:

Enniskillen can now with hindsight be described as one of the turning-points of the Troubles. The deaths of Marie Wilson and ten other people had crucial repercussions for Republicans, for they put an end to Sinn Fein hopes of expansion, especially into the Irish Republic. An IRA spokesman admitted that the outer reaches of Republican support were 'just totally devastated'.

The incident helped initiate a rethink within the IRA and Sinn Fein, and that in turn led to the debate which eventually produced last year's ceasefire. Over the past year Gordon Wilson may have had the comfort of reflecting that the tragedy of Enniskillen planted a seed which, years afterwards, helped his country move from war to peace.

That view is broadly confirmed by sources at the heart of Republicanism. One spokesman told me: 'There are other contributory factors, but it is fair to say that the Enniskillen bombing did not diminish our core support. However, it had a retarding effect on our efforts to build new support, in both parts of Ireland.'

It is easy to understand why Gordon felt so deeply that he had failed in his meeting with the IRA. Though most of his critics tempered their comments with an acknowledgement of his undoubted sincerity, it was widely felt that Gordon had indeed failed, that he had nothing to show for his pains, and that he had been well-meaning but naive, though Republican sources point out that the very fact that the IRA agreed to see him was significant in itself. It is true that he failed to deliver a shift in IRA policy, at the end of his meeting. To that extent all of his many critics were right, and they had a field day.

In a deeper and lasting sense, however, his meeting with the IRA was anything but a failure. The outcome and the hard-line language of the terrorists showed that the IRA seemed incapable of moving with the times, that they held a simplistic 'Brits out' view of a future Irish settlement. They also seemed impervious to pleas for humanity. The meeting showed, too, that they were out of step with all the major parties and with the majority of people in Ireland. In short, they were in step only with themselves as they marched up a cul-de-sac of history, and not along a developing highway in a modern Ireland, North and South.

Later developments, such as the seventeen-month IRA ceasefire which began on 31 August 1994, showed the possibility of some degree of new thinking in the Republican movement, though this ceasefire ended brutally and abruptly with the Canary Wharf bomb in London in February 1996, when two innocent men died and millions of pounds' worth of damage was caused to property. At the time of writing, the situation in Northern Ireland remains volatile, and it is impossible to predict the short-term or long-term future. It is clear, however, that a prolonged debate has been taking place within the IRA and the Republican movement about the use of violence, and there is no doubt that Gordon Wilson's meeting with the IRA leadership (or their representatives), some eighteen months before the IRA ceasefire of 1994 was announced, contributed significantly to that debate – both in public and in private.

Paddy Harte, a friend of Gordon and a member of the Irish Parliament, has long kept his ear to the ground in his native Donegal, and though he is a strong opponent of violence and a dedicated and respected bridge-builder, he knows well the ethos and the thinking of the Republican movement. He believes that Gordon was too impatient in looking for the visible signs of success from his meeting with the IRA, and that he was not sufficiently aware of the hidden dimension. Harte says: 'I talk to many Sinn Fein people in Donegal who have a tremendous admiration for him. He never met these people but he was getting through to them.' It is wrong to suppose that Republicans do not care, he says. 'The flesh and blood of a "Provo" is not terribly different to the flesh and blood of everyone else, and every "hard man" has a vulnerable point.'

Paddy Harte believes that what Gordon said at the meeting, and how he said it, was a discussion point when the IRA spokesmen returned to their colleagues. 'It had to add up to the IRA admiring his courage, and his generosity in being prepared to forgive their associates, and by implication themselves, for killing his daughter.' Gordon, he believes, desperately wanted proof that he had achieved something. 'He was so engrossed in what he was doing that he could not see that he was ploughing land that he was not going to harvest himself. But the harvest will come, and the kind of Ireland he was trying to bring about will be the fruit of that harvest.'

The picture of this still frail man sitting face to face with the associates of Marie's killers, backed by their guns, bombs and armoury, and of Gordon holding nothing more powerful in his hand than the book about his dead daughter, allowed people to make up their own minds about the use of violence and about distinguishing between right and wrong. It also told the world a great deal more about the IRA than it did about Gordon Wilson. He had dared to be a Daniel, he had dared to stand alone, and he had not come away as empty-handed as he had supposed.

13

Darkness Revisited

On a mild November afternoon in 1994, I was walking past Leinster House, the seat of the Irish Parliament in the centre of Dublin. Gordon was parking his distinctive red Mercedes saloon just outside the gates of the building when he spotted me. With typical bonhomie Gordon leapt out of the car and said, 'It's great to see you! Come on in and have a cup of tea with me.' He was in fine form, shaking the hands of passers-by who, recognizing him, as always, greeted him in the street, and he also made time to exchange quips with the uniformed attendants in Leinster House. Once inside, Gordon settled down to enjoy with relish the stories and gossip that we would share over afternoon tea.

Gordon loved the convivial atmosphere of the dining room in Leinster House, and he had the storyteller's knack of embroidering with wit and humour the daily dramas of life in the corridors of political power. As I listened to his animated conversation, I noted privately that at last he seemed to have emerged from the dark tunnel of personal tragedy with renewed strength and vigour. He talked with boyish eagerness about the impending Christmas parliamentary recess, and he was looking forward with great enthusiasm to a holiday he had planned in the Caribbean, with Joan and with Peter and Ingrid and their children.

As I waved goodbye in the dusk of a Dublin evening, I was grateful that Gordon, after all he had come through, seemed on top of the world. But just over a week later, on 7 December, Gordon's world was brutally shattered once again and the entire family was plunged into yet more tragedy and suffering. Peter Wilson was killed almost instantly when his car veered across a busy road and ploughed into an oncoming lorry, just outside Enniskillen. He was 38 years old. For a family which had known such suffering, this latest cruel twist of tragedy was almost beyond belief.

It is still not clear how the accident happened. The lorry driver, who was in a state of shock, said afterwards that the car had suddenly careered across the road straight into his path. There was no way he could stop. Peter's car slammed into the lorry and both were carried a short distance by the impact, ending up in a ditch. Peter was very badly injured and died at the scene a short time later. The drivers of two other vehicles which had been behind Peter did not stop. Either they had been unaware of what had happened, which seems unlikely, or they simply chose to drive on.

It was suggested that Peter had fallen asleep at the wheel after a long drive from Dublin. In fact he had not been in Dublin at all, and was driving home from only a short distance away. He was known to be a fast driver, but there was no evidence that speed caused the accident. Other people, including his mother Joan, believe that he may have fallen asleep at the wheel or may have had a black-out. Yet there was no medical evidence to support this theory. It appears to have been one of those inexplicable and deeply harrowing tragedies which makes people everywhere ask themselves why awful things happen to good people.

Ingrid heard the news just after tea-time on that fateful day. Early that morning she had left Peter in bed at their beautiful house, set on a hillside just off the main road at Pubble, near Enniskillen. It was Wednesday, Peter's day off. By this time he was running an interior design business of his own in Enniskillen, following the sale of the family shop not long after Marie died. Gordon had lost interest in the business, and Peter had decided to go out on his own, first as an agent for a national firm of wholesalers, and later as the proprietor of his own shop. He worked on Saturdays, and on a number of evenings as well to build up the business, and he looked forward to his mid-week break.

Ingrid worked in Enniskillen Model School as a primary schoolteacher, and each Wednesday she took their daughters Eloise and Judith to school – Eloise to Enniskillen Collegiate, and Judith to the Model. It seemed to be just another busy day at school, as they prepared for the Christmas concert. Peter popped into the school at lunch-time to help with the delivery of a musical instrument. Later that afternoon, Ingrid picked up the girls from school and returned to make the evening meal. They were anxious to be home early, as she and Peter had planned to attend a parent-teacher association meeting in the Collegiate, after dropping off the children at a Girls' Brigade meeting at their church. Later their grandmother would pick them up and take them to Cooper Crescent to await their parents' return. Gordon, meanwhile, was busy in Dublin at the Senate.

As she prepared the evening meal, Ingrid began to worry a little about Peter. He was late coming home, and he had not phoned. This was not like him, and she had an uneasy feeling that something might be wrong. At about seven o'clock the doorbell rang, and when she opened the door the first thing she noticed was a large pair of black boots on the door-mat. They were the boots of a policeman, and her heart sank.

Ingrid recalls: 'The policeman said, "Your husband's been involved in an accident." I asked, "Is he dead?" and the policeman replied, "I'm terribly sorry to have to tell you that he's not too good." I froze to the spot. The girls, who had heard the conversation, started to cry. I immediately phoned Joan. I could make no sense of her at all. She just screamed and screamed, and dropped the phone.'

Over at Cooper Crescent, Joan had been preparing special queen cakes for her two little granddaughters and had been looking forward to hearing all about their latest activities. The phone rang, and Ingrid told her the devastating news. She could not believe what she was hearing. Joan remembers Ingrid saying that Peter had had an accident, that his car was under a lorry and that he was badly hurt. 'I threw down the phone and I screamed and screamed. I ran down the hall, up the stairs, along the corridor and back downstairs again. I noticed that the phone was off the hook, so I phoned Ingrid back again, hoping it was not true. She told me what the policeman had said, but I didn't take in a word.'

Joan called Gordon in Dublin. She rang his hotel – Buswells – and she took a long time to get through to his room. Eventually he answered, a little sharply. He had had a long day at the Senate, and he had been relaxing in a bath before dinner. Joan told him the bad news, and he tried to calm her down. 'Don't panic,' he said. 'Just try to tell me as much as you can.' Joan told him all she knew, and said she would go immediately to Peter's house, to be with Ingrid and the children. She told Gordon that she would let him know the latest news about Peter as the evening progressed. By this time their minister, Ivan Carson, and his wife Isa, were at the door. She said, 'I knew by their faces that something terrible had happened.'

The Carsons drove her to Ingrid's house. Joan sat in the back of the car, in a state of turmoil. 'It was like November 1987 all over again. I asked myself, "What's happening to my child? What shape is he in? Is he paralysed? Is he brain-damaged? What will happen to him? What are we going to do?"' She remembers looking at the bare trees on that December evening, with snow and sleet swirling across the front of Peter's house. Inside, there was a scene of utter desolation. Ingrid and the policeman met her inside the front door, and she noticed her two granddaughters crying and huddled together on a chair. Joan looked straight at Ingrid and said, 'Don't tell me Peter is dead!' Ingrid, devastated, and fighting back her tears, replied, 'Granny, I'm afraid so. Peter is dead.' Joan felt all her strength drain away. She could hardly draw breath or think straight. She looked at her widowed daughter-in-law and at her two fatherless grandchildren, and she felt a great wave of desolation sweep over her. Her first coherent thoughts were to contact Gordon, who was waiting in a state of extreme anxiety beside the phone in Dublin. Joan recalls: 'I told him that Peter had died. Gordon was numb with shock, and all I can remember was him saying, "I'll be home." It was dreadful beyond words, because this was the second time I had to tell him that one of our children had died. On that November day in 1987 it was Marie, and now on this December night it was Peter.'

Down in Dublin, Gordon was struggling to take in the shattering news. Another member of the Irish Senate, Madeleine Taylor-Quinn, later recalled the events of that evening: 'I remember that night I was going down the corridor of Kildare House, and Gordon was standing at the door of his office. I walked by and said, "Goodnight, Gordon. How are you?" And he said, "How could I be?" I asked him what was the matter, to which he replied, "My son, my son." I asked him what was wrong with his son and he said, "Peter is dead. He's under a lorry out-side Newtownbutler."

'I could not believe that this man, who was forced in the past to bear such heartbreak, sadness and grief, was again asked to carry another major burden. Yet I had to be impressed – I was the first person to whom he spoke – by the manner, dignity and grace with which he car-ried the news, and the way he subsequently dealt with making arrange-ments to get home to his wife, Joan.'

Gordon's colleagues in Dublin rallied around, in order to get him back to Enniskillen as quickly as possible. He was in no condition to drive, so Alan Dukes, a senior member of the Irish Parliament, drove Gordon's car, and Mrs Taylor-Quinn drove Alan's car. They were met in Virginia, County Cavan – roughly halfway between Dublin and Enniskillen – by Gordon's friend, Crawford Little and his son Peter. Peter drove his own car back to Enniskillen, and Gordon was driven home in his own car by Crawford, who recalls: 'Even at the height of that terrible tragedy, one of the first things Gordon asked me was, "What about the lorry driver. How is he?" This wasn't put on – it was Gordon's natural response.'

Meanwhile, Joan had returned to their home to await Gordon. He arrived shortly before midnight, completely numbed with shock. He looked at her and said, 'Joan, this is some loss we have sustained now.' Gordon's simple, understated response masked a grief and a pain too profound and immense to acknowledge, let alone articulate. He took a cup of tea, but he could not settle until he saw Ingrid, who remembers him coming grief-stricken into her kitchen. 'My mother was also there, and we all cried together. Granda Wilson grieved sore and long.' He embraced his grandchildren, who were also in deep distress, and tried to comfort them as best he could. But words did not come easy, though he had been through the devastation of losing Marie in tragic circum-stances. And even in the midst of tragedy, there were the practicalities. Gordon was a practical man, and his thoughts turned on the post-mortem, to the help that Ingrid would need with arrangements for the funeral and the church service. He also knew that inevitably there would be widespread media coverage, and that the Wilson family would once again be in the public spotlight. And, on top of everything, he was mentally, emotionally and physically exhausted.

There was a much deeper wound, which he and Joan felt keenly. Peter was their eldest child, and after the death of Richard, he was their only son. He was the big man about the house who would look after his parents as they got older. Joan recalls a family lunch on one Remembrance Sunday when she tripped over a mat in the hall of their home. 'Ingrid and Peter came to my rescue, and I remember thinking to myself, "Isn't it great to have a big son like Peter to look after me." But it was not to be, and I have often asked myself why I was not allowed to have my son to take care of me in my old age.'

Peter and Ingrid had a happy marriage, and though they were totally self-sufficient with each other and their children, they played a significant role in the wider family. Joan once said, 'Their marriage was one of the joys of my life.' They met in 1975 when the Wilsons were travelling by boat to France for their summer holiday. Ingrid, then only seventeen, was going to Normandy as part of a students' exchange programme. She had known Joan from the Collegiate school, and she was familiar with Gordon, having visited the Wilsons' shop with her mother. Peter, only a year older, was attracted to Ingrid at first sight, but with a canniness worthy of his father, he tried not to make it too obvious when his parents invited her to join them for a meal on the boat. She had intended later to sleep out on deck because she had not been able to book a berth, but Joan and Gordon insisted that she share a cabin with Julie Anne and Marie.

When Ingrid returned from her exchange studentship in France, she and Peter kept in contact, and in December 1975 she invited him to her school's formal dance. The romance blossomed, and they remained in close contact even when Ingrid went to Stranmillis College in Belfast, where Julie Anne had also trained as a teacher. As soon as Ingrid finished her course she and Peter became engaged, and they were married on 2 August 1980, the day of Joan and Gordon's silver wedding anniversary. Peter and Ingrid lived initially in Joan's old home at Pubble, and within a year they moved into a spacious and beautiful new house on land just behind the original family dwelling. In July 1983

Eloise was born, and Judith arrived some two years later. Life for Peter and Ingrid was very happy, despite the pressures and demands of family life. There was hardly a cloud in their sky, apart from the premature death of Ingrid's father at the age of 59.

Marie's death in 1987 was devastating for Ingrid and Peter, as it was for the whole family. They had both been close to Marie, and the manner of her death was particularly hard to bear. Peter did not share his father's sentiments, though he recognized the nobility of his words. Ingrid says: 'Peter never forgave the bombers. The fact that he never knew who they were really got to him. He could never accept that he might be rubbing shoulders with these people, and the fact that no one was ever charged was something which really hurt him.' Peter, with typical loyalty to his father, kept his thoughts to himself. Like Julie Anne, he never approved of the media's intrusion into their lives, but he accepted that his father was reacting to the tragedy in his own way. Peter also believed that his father's public stance of forgiveness lost him business, but if that was the price Gordon had to pay for taking that stance, so be it.

Peter's relationship with his father was a mixture of love, admiration and awe. Peter was proud of his father, but he felt that he was not given enough responsibility in business. Yet he never crossed Gordon, or faced him head-on. Gordon, for his part, was extremely proud of Peter and, according to Joan, he would have given him the coat off his back. They had a very strong and close relationship, but like many a father and son, they did not always show their emotions openly to each other. Gordon's father had been the same with him, and the habit lingered on. Ingrid says: 'Peter and Gordon were very different characters. Peter was much softer, and I would say he was far too nice. Peter looked like his Dad, but he was much more like his mother. Gordon had a hard streak, although he could also be very warm and generous. But when he looked straight at you, he really did look at you. I think Peter was a little in awe of him.'

Peter, however, had his strong points. He was gracious, charming and a good talker in his own way. Like his father, he could be stubborn, and he had many a set-to with his mother, who did not give in so easily to him as Gordon. Gordon could be a tough and demanding boss to Peter, but he was, first and foremost, an indulgent father. His mother loved and encouraged his gentler side and his creativity. He used to talk to her a great deal about his interior design business, and about colour combinations and furnishings. He was constantly attentive, and made a point of checking that Joan had everything she needed. When Gordon was away in Dublin on Senate business, or elsewhere on speaking engagements, Peter always made a point of staying in close touch with his mother. His parents loved him deeply, and his sudden death was an irreparable loss.

Julie Anne also felt his loss keenly. She was not as close to Peter as she had been to Marie, but she grieved for her brother and for Ingrid and the children. She says: 'It all seemed so unfair, and I could not bear to think about Ingrid on her own, or about the girls without their father. I grieved for my parents, who had lost not one but three children, which must have been a terrible blow for them. When Peter died, I said to Dad, "I'm so sorry that the others have been taken from you. Maybe if you had had your choice you would have wanted Peter or Marie to have been left alive, rather than me." He gave me one of those looks which meant that he had nothing to say. It was a silly thing for me to ask, because there is no answer to that sort of a question. As a parent you know that you love all your children, not in the same way, but when one of them dies it means that a part of you dies as well. That was what Dad was trying to tell me with that look in his eyes, but he was too far spent to put it into words. I grieved for him, and I was so sorry for him, and I loved him so much, but at that point no one could help him. His loss was deep, and so profound. I hugged him, but I felt that he had nothing left inside – he had nothing left to give.'

On the night of Peter's death, Gordon and Joan returned to their home at Cooper Crescent well after midnight, but they were in great distress and they had a sleepless night. Joan says: 'It was the same as the night Marie died. We cried, we tossed and turned, we got up and walked around the house. We could get no peace anywhere. We had been through it before, but that was no comfort. We felt the same pain, and the shock and the deep sense of loss. I prayed to the Lord for help, because I knew that without him I could not get through what seemed to be a nightmare but which was terribly real. I thought of some of the words of Psalm 56: "put thou my tears into thy bottle: are they not in thy book?"'

Yet even as the Wilsons grieved in private, the story of the latest tragedy to hit the family was making headline news, locally and nationally. Peter's death was the lead story in most of the radio and television bulletins, and print and broadcasting reporters were filing news stories and preparing special feature reports. The *Daily Mail* front-page headline told the story: 'New grief for Gordon Wilson – terrorists killed his daughter, now his son dies in a car crash.' The *Belfast Telegraph* noted sadly in its editorial, 'It is one of life's unfathomable ironies that tragedy often strikes at people whose contribution to society is nothing but good.' The family decided not to talk to the media, as Gordon had done after Marie's death, but instead Gordon issued a general statement: 'Joan and I and our immediate family are deeply shocked and saddened at the sudden and tragic death of our son Peter. We are very much aware of the loss his death will mean to the family circle, and in particular to his wife Ingrid and their two little girls, Eloise and Judith.' A relative told one enquiring reporter, 'It is a private matter for Gordon and his family. They want to be left alone to grieve in peace.' To be fair, the media did not intrude directly on their privacy, though there was a large media presence outside the Darling Street Methodist Church for Peter's funeral.

It took place on a dark, wet and sombre Saturday, just two weeks before Christmas. On the way to the funeral, my wife and I called in to Cooper Crescent to see Gordon and Joan, at their request. Both were composed and dignified, though grieving deeply, but Gordon paced up and down the kitchen with even more restless energy than usual. He addressed an open question to me: 'What do you think we should do? We have booked a holiday to the Caribbean at Christmas, but Joan and the girls don't want to go, although I think we should. The ladies will need the break after all this. What would your view be?' I stalled for time and said, 'Gordon, just let that go now. It will sort itself out in the next few days.' But he shook his head, unconvinced by the answer, and walked off to greet another visitor who had come through the front door. When he left the kitchen, I looked at Joan and said, 'It's Gordon who needs the break, not you and the girls.' Joan nodded her head in agreement. 'I know that,' she said. 'But he doesn't want to admit it.'

The Methodist Church was packed for Peter's funeral, and the overflow congregation sat in the church hall. Before the service began, President Mary Robinson privately met Ingrid and the children, as well as Julie Anne and Gordon and Joan. Joan says: 'Gordon was very fond of President Robinson, and thought highly of her. She was sympathetic and gracious, and she had a steadying, calming effect on us.' The presence of the President of Ireland was symbolic of the deep affection which the Irish people felt for Gordon and his family, and also their sense of sympathy on this latest tragedy. There was an impressive attendance by senior politicians from Dublin, including the Tanaiste (Deputy Prime Minister), Dick Spring, who was also the Irish Foreign Minister and Labour Party leader; John Bruton, the then Fine Gael leader, and his colleague Austin Currie, a Northerner who was close to Gordon and helpful to him in Leinster House; Mary Harney, leader of the Progressive Democrats; and a number of Senators, including Dr Mary Henry, who had been a close colleague of Gordon. They had a special bond in that her father had once been employed by Gordon's father in the Manorhamilton shop. The Irish Prime Minister, Albert Reynolds, was unable to attend, and he was represented by a military aide-de-camp. The attendance of so many leading Irish politicians was a particular tribute to Gordon, because at that time Irish political life was undergoing a prolonged upheaval which soon afterwards led to a change in government.

A number of leading politicians from Northern Ireland were also present, including Michael Ancram, who represented the British Government, and also Dr Joe Hendron of the predominantly Catholic and Nationalist Social Democratic and Labour Party. Gordon also noted privately, with great disappointment, that there was no significant formal representation from the Official Unionist Party. (Those who do not know the subtleties of social and political life in Ireland should note that the absence of an individual or a group at a funeral is often as significant as their presence.)

The service was conducted by the Minister, the Reverend Ivan Carson, who spoke movingly about Peter's life and family and his contribution to the church. He described the poignant moment when the lorry driver involved in the accident met Ingrid, Joan and Gordon. 'They shared their feelings of loss and put their arms around each other and cried.' Peter's uncle, the Reverend Dr Hedley Plunkett, read one of the lessons, and the service itself was a revelation to many of the Southern visitors, who would not have had the opportunity in the Irish Republic to attend a Methodist service with such a large congregation. It was part of a rich Protestant culture which is not readily accessible in the Republic, where Protestants are very much in a minority. The singing at Methodist services in the North can be most uplifting, and one senior civil servant from Dublin, Walter Kirwan (Secretary-General of the Forum), was particularly moved by the hymn 'Thine be the Glory'. When his wife Anne died tragically a few weeks later, this was one of the hymns which he chose for her funeral, and he asked a colleague to bring along some members of a Protestant choir from a Dublin church nearby to share in singing it at his wife's funeral service in a Catholic church. That is the kind of human story which would have touched Peter's heart.

Despite the singing at Peter's funeral and the words of Gospel hope, it was a crushingly sad occasion. There was a sense in the church of a terrible loss, as Ingrid and her children, and Peter's parents and sister, and his brother-in-law walked down the aisle behind his coffin. Outside they were met by a barrage of press and television cameras as the media recorded the funeral for the evening bulletins and the next day's Sunday newspapers.

Gordon and many of the mourners, including senior Dublin politicians, walked behind the coffin in the rain to a local cemetery, while a large number of the other mourners went into the church hall for a cup of tea, provided by the hard-working ladies of the church. Gordon later returned, and he and Joan greeted as many people as they could. It was in itself an historic gathering, with Irish Government ministers and senior Opposition politicians, the vast majority of them Catholics, rubbing shoulders with Protestants in a Methodist Church hall in Northern

Ireland. Even in the shadow of death there was a unique and special mix of Northern and Southern, and Protestant and Catholic cultures, as human beings from all parts of Ireland shared in the sorrow of a family which had known so much suffering.

For Ingrid, above all, it was totally heart-breaking. She was calm and dignified as she held her two daughters close to her, and as she greeted many of the mourners, most of them complete strangers. But she was churning inside as she thought of the irreparable loss of the young man in his prime who had been her childhood sweetheart, her husband, and the father of her children. No words and no sympathy could assuage her grief, or heal the wounds. The Sunday papers, which widely reported the funeral, unwittingly added to her pain with headlines such as 'Nations united by father's grief'. 'What about *our* grief?' Ingrid cried to herself. 'Peter had a wife and children too!' Gordon and Joan understood, but they could do nothing about the headlines. This family, united in the deepest of private grief, had once again to live out their suffering in the full glare of the public spotlight. Their darkness, revisited, could never be totally private.

Each member of the family grieved in their own way, but whereas Joan and Ingrid could weep together and console each other, Gordon's grief was intense and private. He found such grief difficult to express, and when he did talk about it, he used the minimum of words. Perhaps he was unable to communicate it even to himself, and much less to accept it. Julie Anne's instinct that he had nothing left to give may have been close to the truth. Was Peter's death the beginning of his own end? Somewhere, deep down and unknown even to himself, had he given up?

14

Death on a Summer's Day

The days following Peter Wilson's death were bleak and lonely beyond description as the family tried to come to terms with this latest, and enormous, loss. It was especially poignant during the approach to Christmas, when so many others were looking forward to sharing and celebrating this special family season. And there was the question of whether they should all go away. The planned holiday in the Caribbean seemed inappropriate in many ways, and yet Joan remembered how a holiday had been such a healing experience after Marie's death. After thinking it over carefully, they went to the Caribbean for Christmas and the New Year, and it proved to be the right decision. Joan says: 'We got the break we all so badly needed. There was time to rest, to reflect and to try to get things into perspective, and the girls loved the new sights and sounds and the excitement of it all. Once again I felt the healing of just being beside the ocean. I was also able to share with Ingrid, and I knew that Gordon desperately needed a rest.'

They returned to Enniskillen in early January to face the harsh reality of life without Peter. Gordon and Joan had gone through the trauma of Marie's death, yet this time it was no easier. Joan says: 'We knew a bit more about coping, about the things which hurt and which cut deeply, but we never really overcame the pain of losing Peter. We would talk about it together, and Gordon would say, "Even for Christians, life is no bed of roses. This is something we will have to get through, with the help of God."' They received thousands of letters, as they had done after Marie's death, and each was replied to personally. This in itself was a kind of therapy, and they received inspiration and comfort from those who had taken the trouble to write. The letters came from all over the British Isles, and from many other parts of the world. Gordon remarked on the particularly large number of letters from Wales, where he had made many friends through speaking engagements. They also felt greatly supported by the prayers of many people. Joan says: 'It was an almost tangible thing, like a solid wall of support bearing us up. I've always believed in the power of prayer, but this was something you could almost put out your hand and touch.' Sadly, there were a number of abusive letters, including one which claimed that Peter's death was a judgement of God on Gordon for taking his seat in the Forum. Such letters were burned.

Together Joan and Gordon visited the cemetery where Peter and Marie were buried, and they would grieve there, often in private. Sometimes Gordon would go to Peter's grave alone, and he would come back to Joan to tell her where he had been. He would say, 'Joan, I've been down to see Peter's grave, and it's a very sad sight,' the simplicity of his words again concealing the immensity of his loss. Gordon was particularly cut up when he visited Ingrid and the girls in their home. Joan says: 'Most times he would come back in tears, and say to me, "Joan, it's awfully lonely down there for Ingrid and the girls. I can't bear to think of those three women on their own."' (He often referred to Ingrid and his granddaughters as 'the three women'.)

Gordon was a tower of strength to Ingrid, in many practical ways. He was good at sorting out Peter's complex legal and financial affairs, and providing the kind of advice which she needed as a young widow faced with bringing up two children. But he was on shaky ground emotionally. Ingrid recalls: 'Granda Wilson was great at giving me sound financial advice, but all I wanted was to have my husband back. I would say, "I don't care how much I will have to live on – all I want is Peter!" He would say, "That's all very well, but you can't bring him back. We all have to face reality." He seemed so hard, but he was doing what was right. The truth was, he couldn't handle it emotionally himself, just like Peter was after Marie's death. He could never get it out into the open. He talked, to a certain degree, but not fully. Granda could never say, "I'm really sorry." He just couldn't handle it that way.'

Ingrid and Joan were better able to deal with their emotions, perhaps because they were women. Ingrid says: 'Granny Wilson and I could talk together and cry together and console one another. We both had lost someone unique to us, and we could share that loss in different ways. Like Peter did, I admire Granny Wilson tremendously. She is so strong, like a rock, and she holds us all together. Peter once asked her, after Marie died, "How do you have such faith?" And she replied, "I'm 30 years down life's road from you!" In 30 years' time I would be happy to have a faith like Granny Wilson's.'

Despite her trauma and loss, Ingrid's Christian faith remained solid. She says: 'I get good days and bad days. I still ask questions, I still think, "Why me?" I hate people saying, "This is God's will." I don't believe that God creates evil or makes people suffer in this way. I still believe that there was a reason for Peter's death, that there is something real after this life. I believe that, more than ever.'

Gordon responded to Peter's death in his own way, which was to work as hard as he could, to try to blot out the pain. His family, friends and colleagues all noted a marked increase in the already frenetic pace of his life-style. But the cracks began to show. Julie Anne recalls: 'He went into top gear, and we could not make him stay at home or take things easy. When Peter died he cried a lot, in front of everyone. He would say, "We have lost Marie, and now Peter. We will never get over this." He said it over and over, and it used to kill me.'

Julie Anne believes that he really never recovered from Peter's death. It was something so deep and so fundamental that his reserves of emotional strength and courage could not cope with the strain. She says: 'In one sense he almost "went mad", because he simply could not say "No" to any invitation to speak and to travel. I believe that in the end he was no longer in control.' Joan agrees that he was working far too hard, but believes that he was in better shape physically than in the period after Marie died.

'He had learned how to try to cope with grief after Marie's death and, because of the bomb, he was very poorly physically. But in the intervening years he had become stronger, he had put on weight, and he had learned, like me, about dealing with the pain of losing a child. It was almost as if he had learned to come to terms with Marie's death. But Peter's death, so sudden and brutal in its own way, knocked him off his stride completely. However, he was managing to hold on to his schedule. It was keeping his mind off other things, and provided he had enough relaxation at weekends, I felt that we were managing to deal with the worst of the suffering.'

Gordon was setting himself a punishing pace, and even if part of his hidden motive – perhaps hidden even to himself – was to try to stop thinking about Peter, he was also anxious to take every opportunity to promote reconciliation. The Provisional IRA and Loyalist ceasefires were holding, but the political process was becoming bogged down through recriminations and a lack of trust on all sides. It was imperative that the voice of reconciliation was heard loud and clear. In these months of his frenetic activity, Gordon was making a valuable contribution to the Senate and to the Forum for Peace and Reconciliation. Equally important, he was presenting on television and other media, with sincerity and eloquence, the argument for reconciliation, and also he was telling Marie's story to audiences all around the British Isles. Though he may literally have worked himself to death, not a moment or an opportunity was wasted to argue the case for taking the gun and the bomb out of Irish politics and for working for peace.

Though Gordon pushed himself and others hard, his family life was undoubtedly a refuge and a strength. When he came home from Dublin, full of Senate business and talking about well-known people and the 'personalities' he had met, Joan and Julie Anne were able to help him to relax and to keep his feet on the ground. He adored all his grandchildren, and one of the joys of his life was the birth of his grandsons Scott and Timothy. Shortly after Marie's death, Julie Anne had started going out with John Hassard, a young local man who worked in the motor trade, and they were married in July 1991. Joan says: 'This brought great happiness to all of us. After the terrible years following Marie's death, it seemed that our lives had taken on a semblance of the normality of other families.'

Julie Anne says: 'He spoiled the boys outrageously. He used to take Scott for a drive in his red Mercedes and then allow him to place his hands on the steering wheel as the child sat in his lap. I thought that this was terrible, but Dad wouldn't listen to me! Timothy was too young to remember him, but Scott absolutely loved him. One day we pulled into the petrol station where Dad often took him, and out of the blue he said to me, "Poor ol' Granda is dead!"'

Gordon's colleagues and friends saw that he was driving himself too hard. Aisling Maguire, his secretary-assistant in Dublin, says: 'After Peter's death, I could see a kind of desperation in the way he worked. He had an almost frenzied energy in the way he tried to keep busy, to stop him brooding on his grief.' Albert Reynolds also noticed this frantic activity. He says: 'I used to tell Gordon that he was driving himself too hard. I remember him asking me for the shortest route from Enniskillen to Tullamore, because he was aware that I knew the area well. Every time I met him, he was going somewhere or coming from somewhere, and I said to him on a couple of occasions, "Gordon, you are doing a fine job, you are reconciliation personified, but slow down a bit. None of us is getting any younger."' Mary Harney, leader of the Progressive Democrats, noticed it too. 'All that travelling probably killed him, in the end. The man was exhausted, he worked so hard.' Christine Smith, his editor, met him in London shortly after Peter's death. 'On the surface he was his usual, sociable self, but he could not talk about Peter at all. There was a relentlessness about him, which seemed to be his way of coping.'

Other friends noticed the same pattern. Our friendship continued after the publication of the book about Marie, and he would occasionally ring me up and talk about his latest journey, or speech, or broadcast, but he would never talk about Peter. When you have written a book about a man, you get to know him, and I believe that I knew Gordon well. Peter's death was driving him on, but it was the one subject we never mentioned. I wanted to talk to him about Peter, but he never raised the subject, and I felt I couldn't. But the agony of it was there, all the time. We were both very busy in the months after Peter died, and perhaps he might have talked about it if we had been able to spend a day or an evening together, or if I had been around Leinster House on those evenings when he needed company and had more time to open up.

The spring months passed, and Gordon felt ready to think about the invitation he had received from an editor to write a second book. Again, he wanted me to work with him on it. Early in June he called me, and we arranged to spend a day together to talk about the project. The first free day that suited both of us, and our families, was a Saturday in the middle of August. Two weeks after the phone-call, Gordon was dead.

Gordon died from a stroke on the morning of 27 June 1995. The gregarious man who was known to so many people and who cherished the company of others died alone in his own home. Joan was away in Galway, and Julie Anne was travelling from Moira to Enniskillen to meet up with him. Though the family knew that he had been driving himself hard, there had been no signs that he was unwell.

The previous couple of days had been strenuous. On the Sunday Joan had left with a party of musicians and singers from two Enniskillen schools. They were due to give performances in the Galway area, as part of a cross-community school project under the auspices of Education for Mutual Understanding. Gordon dropped Joan off at St Michael's School, and she reminded him that she had specially stocked the freezer with food and that there would be more than enough for him to eat. She knew that he hated being alone in the house, and that he was likely, as usual, to go to a friend's house rather than cook for himself and eat alone – which is exactly what he did! But she made sure that he was provided for. It was a beautiful summer's day. They embraced, and she promised to phone him that evening.

In the afternoon, Gordon drove across the Irish border to the holiday resort of Rossnowlagh in County Donegal, where Peter and Ingrid had kept a holiday home, and where Ingrid, her mother and the girls were staying. This was the first time since Peter's death that he had been able to face visiting Rossnowlagh. He and Ingrid and the children went to the beach and played on that hot and sunny afternoon, during what was one of the best summers in Ireland for many years. On the way there he had been caught in a traffic-jam, and this had irritated him greatly. Gordon liked keeping on the move, and he could not bear being held up. That evening he drove back again in heavy traffic, and he made a mental note that he would never let this happen again. Ingrid's mother returned to Enniskillen with him, and she noticed that he took a wrong turning. But she made no comment. Gordon's mind was preoccupied with what had the potential to be yet another tragedy for the Wilson family.

Earlier that day his son-in-law, John Hassard, had come off his motorbike at speed and was unconscious and in intensive care in the Erne Hospital in Enniskillen. Julie Anne was beside herself with worry, and Gordon had gone to the hospital to comfort her. When Joan phoned from Galway, Gordon told her about John, but advised her that there was no need to come back at that stage. The next morning John regained consciousness, and began to make a rapid recovery. Julie Anne recalls: 'Dad came to see him, and he was so relieved that John was all right. He was a bit annoyed, too, that John had caused us all such worry, and he gave him one look which said it all. John felt suitably guilty!' The motorbike was a write-off and John decided not to replace it.

On the Monday afternoon John was allowed out of hospital, and Julie Anne borrowed her mother's car to take him back to their home in Moira. She was to return the car the next morning, and Gordon would take her back to Moira on his way to Belfast, where he had a 'Spirit of Enniskillen' meeting in Belfast Castle on the Tuesday evening. But on that Monday afternoon, Gordon was finding the heat unbearable, and he decided to have a lie down. Before she left for Moira, Julie Anne looked into his room. She says: 'He was absolutely out for the count. It was uncannily like a "dry run" for what I found the next day.' Later on the Monday, Ingrid and the girls called in to see Gordon. Ingrid says: 'He seemed rather dazed. He told us he had gone for a nap and he couldn't believe that he had slept for several hours.' Shortly after tea-time Ingrid and the girls left Cooper Crescent. As they pulled away, Gordon went out into the road to wave a fond farewell. This was unusual for him, and Eloise commented, 'It looks as if Granda is waving goodbye to us.' In the evening he was invited to dinner at the home of his secretary, Michelle Kennedy, and her husband. Not being a man for half measures, he brought along a whole salmon as a gift. Gordon was always good company, but his hosts thought he seemed rather tired.

Gordon spoke to Joan and Julie Anne on the phone later that evening, and he spent the rest of the evening quietly at home. He had plenty to occupy his mind, as he was still in the middle of a busy speaking and writing schedule, and was preparing for an eagerly awaited holiday in South Africa. At around 8.30 on the Tuesday morning, Joan rang him from Galway. She says: 'He seemed in good form. He told me the latest news about John, and I was so pleased and relieved about his progress. I told him about our music-making in Galway, and he was interested in all the details. He said that Julie Anne was coming down later that morning, and that after lunch they would set off for Moira, prior to his engagement in Belfast. We talked about ordinary family things, and we were both looking forward to getting back to Cooper Crescent after our various travels. Neither of us had the slightest inkling that this was to be our last conversation.'

An hour later, Aisling Maguire rang Gordon from Dublin on routine business concerning the Forum for Peace and Reconciliation. By midmorning, Julie Anne had left Moira in her mother's car, headed for Enniskillen. The heat was oppressive. She arrived at Cooper Crescent shortly before noon, to find the house wide open but feeling strangely empty. Her father usually had coffee with a few friends in the town each morning, but she reckoned that even if he was late coming back, he would not have left the door and windows open.

The house was pleasantly cool after the intense heat outside, and the curtains were blowing in a gentle breeze. Julie Anne hesitated, and then went and sat in a deck-chair in the garden, and thought about what to do next. Perhaps her father had nipped across to see a neighbour, or had gone to buy petrol and had not bothered to lock up the house. But the longer she sat, the more uneasy she became. Suddenly she remembered seeing her father out for the count the day before and began to picture the unimaginable. She said to herself, 'Calm down, Julie Anne, you're losing your nerve. Everything is all right.' But the nagging fear grew, and she went back into the house to search for her father. She came to his bedroom, and her heart sank. He was lying on the bed, on his side. He was fully clothed, and wearing his shoes. Only his glasses were missing, and they were on a table beside the bed. He looked as if he had lain down for a short rest, but there was something disturbingly different about that familiar figure in repose.

Julie Anne recalls vividly: 'As soon as I saw him, I knew he was dead. I felt a sense of dread, as I said to myself, "There's no Mum, no Marie, no Peter here – what am I going to do?" Then those worries were banished to the back of my mind, and I felt a great peace coming from Dad. I said to myself, "If you could choose your way of dying, this is it."

'I had not seen such a peace on his face for a long time, not since before Marie died. He looked so content. I am sure that he did not want to die, but he could not have kept on going the way he was. And I thought of him dying perhaps when he was driving the car, or maybe finding him lying by the roadside. By that time I was outwardly as calm as a breeze, which seems amazing, in the circumstances. The deaths of Marie and Peter had been so shocking, and so brutal. By contrast, Dad's death was so natural. I felt relieved that I was there with him, and that nobody else had to tell me. It was a great sense of relief and of release, and I found that coming from Dad to me.'

Julie Anne stayed in the room for a few minutes, silently looking at her dead father, and then went out to call for help from the neighbours. They rallied round, as they always did, and soon the police were asking their colleagues in Galway to find Joan and tell her the news of Gordon's death.

At mid-day she and all the others from Enniskillen were in the final stages of preparing for the lunch-time public concert in the new Eyre Square shopping centre. Joan recalls the first couple of items, including a beautiful rendering of the hit song 'The Music of the Night' from *The Phantom of the Opera*, which still reminds her vividly of the events of that day, each time it is played. She was in the middle of a trio of items with the Collegiate Choir, and at the end the conductor, Bob Quick, approached Joan, held her hands and told her directly, 'I'm sorry to give you terrible news. Gordon has died at home.'

The concert was abandoned, and Joan remembers being taken by Bob Quick and another friend, Evelyn Hassard, down to an office in the shopping complex. She recalls that many hands were stretched out to her to express condolences. Someone gave her strong tea, but her hands were shaking so much that she could hardly hold the teacup. She says: 'The police in Galway were very kind, and I remember them passing me messages from Julie Anne and from the Royal Ulster Constabulary. They told me that Gordon had passed away peacefully and that he had not suffered. That was a comfort to me. I was still disbelieving, but I shall never forget the kindness shown to me.'

Joan collected her suitcase, which Evelyn had packed hurriedly, and the police drove her towards the Irish border. On the way back in the police car, Joan heard the stones rattling the bodywork from the hot, dusty road, and she could feel a cool breeze coming in from the window. She began to think ahead. 'I said to myself, "This is another funeral to plan", and for an instant I thought, "Oh, well, Peter will be able to help." Then I almost cried out loud, "Peter has gone too!" I knew yet again that my help and strength came from the Lord, and he had never failed me yet.'

Joan was met at Claremorris by Julie Anne, who had been driven there by the same friend, Peter Little, who had driven Gordon part of the way back from Dublin when Peter died. A next-door neighbour, Edna Young, was also with them. Mother and daughter embraced, and Julie Anne said: 'Mum, he didn't suffer. He is with Marie and Peter now. He is happy.' Joan nodded in the midst of her tears and held tightly on to Julie Anne's hand. She said: 'We're on our own now. With the help of the Lord, we'll have to be strong.'

Not until Joan arrived back at Cooper Crescent did reality sink in. The house was filled with friends and neighbours. They were full of warmth and sympathy, as they held out their hands or hugged Joan and Julie Anne. Faxes and phone calls were coming in, and flowers began arriving. But the most important person of all was missing. Joan says: 'There was no welcome from Gordon. When I normally came home and he was there, I would get a big smile and a cheery greeting: "Well, Mum, how did it go? Come on in. I'm glad to see you home." This time he wasn't there. I felt helpless, weary, unwilling to face the grief, the publicity, the funeral and the aftermath. It was so hard.' She knew that she had to bear up, not only to try to keep her own composure but also to help the others. But deep down she wondered how she would ever cope. Gordon had always been there for her. In human terms she felt so totally alone. She wanted it all to pass like a dream, but the nightmare was only too real. How could she ever accept that Gordon was dead?

She dreaded seeing him lying dead on their bed, but she could not bear the thought of not seeing him. 'Julie Anne tried to protect me, and told me not to go in. But I had to see him. Once I was inside the room, the sense of dread left me. He was lying there, with a great air of peace about him. As soon as I saw him, the words came to me, "Mission accomplished". I said to him, "Gordon, dear, you have done your best. You have given your all for peace and reconciliation." I prayed to God for strength, and I remembered how he had helped me in the past.

'I left the room, but I went back in again, on my own. I stood quietly at the side of the bed and looked at Gordon for several minutes, and thought of the 39 years we had shared together, and all that we had gone through. Like Gordon had done after the deaths of Marie and Peter, I had to face the future, but he would no longer be by my side. It was our last private moment together. I thanked God for all that Gordon had been to me and to our children, and for all he had done for peace and reconciliation. I had to struggle on, with the help of Julie Anne and the others, but now he was at peace. He had passed on to something greater, in the nearer presence of the Lord. His mission was truly accomplished. I whispered a quiet farewell and kissed Gordon's face.' Joan turned away from the bed and went slowly downstairs to face the future.

Despite the pain and anguish of losing a lifelong partner and a supportive, loving husband, Gordon's death seemed to strengthen Joan, in contrast to the deaths of Marie and Peter, which had torn her apart and ravaged her inner peace. She would miss him terribly, and she dreaded the prospect of facing life on her own. Yet she could look back on Gordon's long life, in contrast to the brutally early deaths of Marie and Peter, and she could thank God that despite all of Gordon's pain and heartbreak, he had been able to achieve so much. This brought her comfort in her latest bereavement, and in a life with more personal tragedies than anyone should be asked to bear, she had learned how to cope in the hardest of schools.

15

Mission Accomplished

The news of Gordon's death on the morning of Tuesday 27 June 1995 was making headlines from early afternoon, and by tea-time it was being featured widely on television and radio programmes in Northern Ireland and throughout the United Kingdom, in the Irish Republic and overseas. Newspaper reporters, editorial writers and columnists were busy preparing their articles for the next day's editions. Gordon Wilson had made headlines in the last eight years of his life, and he was making headlines in death.

The Queen, through a Buckingham Palace spokesman, paid tribute to his 'depth of forgiveness and lack of bitterness'. President Mary Robinson said that Gordon's legacy was important and enduring: 'His own personal courage in the face of the devastating tragedies that he experienced in recent years was, and still is, an invaluable source of inspiration for all who have been affected by the violence of the past 25 years.'

There were tributes from colleagues and friends in the Irish and British Parliaments, and from broadcasting studios in Belfast, Dublin, London and elsewhere. Sometimes such tributes can seem a little stereotyped, but those ones about Gordon were warm, spontaneous and authentic – just like the man himself. Prime Minister John Major noted Gordon's 'remarkable and in many ways unique contribution' and said, 'I think there would be no better legacy than to continue what he sought to do and to carry the peace process forward.' The Irish Prime Minister, John Bruton, said that Gordon had shown all Irish people, North and South, how 'one can forgive great hurt and seek reconciliation by living a constructive and positive life'. The Irish Deputy Prime Minister, Dick

Spring, said: 'He set an example which we must continue to follow, and he left a legacy which will never be forgotten.'

Even Gordon's political critics found it possible to say a kind word, without compromising their expressed differences with a man whom they thought well-meaning but politically misguided and naive. Ken Magennis, Gordon's local Westminster MP, said that he had set a wonderful example of the power of forgiveness, and while he believed that Gordon's commitment to the peace process was sometimes naively expressed, there was no doubting his sincerity. Sammy Wilson, a member of the hard-line Democratic Unionists, who had nevertheless impressed Gordon and Joan by his kindness in helping them with their luggage at a conference they had attended together, paid tribute and said that while he believed Gordon was misguided in some of his actions and comments, he was utterly genuine.

Mitchell McLaughlin, the National Chairman of Sinn Fein, extended condolences to Joan and said: 'It was his forgiving nature when he lost his daughter Marie that set the scene for people to re-examine what was going on in Northern Ireland.'

Colin Parry recalled Gordon's visit after the death of his son in the Warrington bombing: 'His words were more valuable than anything that had been said before, or after.'

In both houses of the Irish Parliament, differences were put aside as members acknowledged the loss not merely of a political colleague, but of a friend. Senator Maurice Manning, the leader of the Senate, said that everything about Gordon was big, generous, Christian and loving. He taught everyone how to forgive, how to live together and how to rebuild: '"He spoke for the ordinary, decent people who wanted a way out of lives dominated by hatred, bombing and murder, and for those people he spoke eloquently, passionately and honestly. His presence did make a difference. History will be kind to Gordon Wilson.'

Albert Reynolds was visibly shocked as he paid tribute in the Irish Parliament, and said it was difficult to understand how the Wilson family were asked to bear such an unbearable burden of tragedy. Gordon had accepted his cross and had wished to share with everybody his innermost thoughts of forgiveness and reconciliation. Austin Currie, a

Minister of State and a fellow Ulsterman, said: 'He worked too hard and he committed himself too much, but that was in the nature of the true Christian gentleman he was.' Mary Harney, Leader of the Progressive Democrats, said: 'If we leave no stone unturned in seeking to consolidate the peace process, then we shall have paid a great tribute to an extraordinary man and a great colleague.' Proinsias De Rossa, Leader of the Democratic Left, said that Gordon was truly a remarkable man whose courage and resilience were an inspiration to people of all religions, of none, and to those of virtually every political persuasion.

Letters and messages of sympathy arrived from many people in British public life, including the Princess of Wales and the Foreign Secretary, Douglas Hurd. The tributes from ordinary people were no less appreciated. Letters poured in to Joan and her family from all over Ireland, the United Kingdom, Europe, North America, Australia, South Africa, New Zealand, Saudi Arabia and even Wagga Wagga in Australia! Some were typed, many were hand-written, and their simplicity and sincerity were heart-warming. It was fitting that an 'ordinary' man of the people like Gordon could inspire so many 'ordinary' people to respond in such a way.

Don Byard from Thurles in County Tipperary wrote that he had never met Gordon, but like so many of the ordinary citizens of Ireland, he had become familiar with his 'gentle face and sincere voice' offering a note of sanity and hope to all in troubled times:

> Yesterday, when I heard of his death on the news, I genuinely felt as if I had lost a friend, indeed a close friend who articulated all that was good and noble, and shared ideals and set standards that we should love to be able to match, for forgiveness and reconciliation. When the history books record the great deeds as well as the outrages of this century on this island, I know that the name of Gordon Wilson will occupy a proud place as the finest example of what one man can do so eloquently and bravely to bring us to our senses and show us a better way.

Shayne Mary Mitchell from Bedfordshire remarked how Gordon was criticized for being 'naive' in meeting the IRA:

> I found such criticism dispiriting, it seemed a deeply courageous and hopeful act. And I couldn't see what was wrong with naivety anyway – much good has come from 'naive' actions. And saints, by most criteria, are naive. But now it is too late to write to your husband. I admired him so very much; I found him a man of such integrity and charity.

David Bloomer, who worked in the drapery business in Lisburn, wrote describing Gordon's kindness to him from the first day he called into Wilson's shop forty years earlier:

> Some people found it hard to understand his wonderful words of forgiveness when Marie died, but I always told the story of how I arrived one morning in the middle of the first day of the Wilson's 'Sale'. Gordon said, 'David, it's very good of you to call all the way from Belfast. We'll get you a cup of tea, and get you on your way.' Not another retailer in Ireland would have treated me with such courtesy and thoughtfulness, and I have never forgotten it.

Similar tributes arrived for months afterwards. Joan was touched and strengthened by such a spontaneous outpouring of affection and respect for Gordon and by such care and concern for her family and herself. But in the immediate aftermath of Gordon's death there were sombre and urgent practicalities to be attended to, including the funeral. Joan had more than enough experience of such matters, but she was greatly helped by her minister, Ivan Carson. She planned a simple service of thanksgiving, and chose several of Gordon's favourite hymns, including 'Jesus, lover of my soul', 'Love Divine, all loves excelling', and the hymn which was sung at Peter's funeral, 'Thine be the glory, risen, conquering Son'.

On the evening before the funeral, Gordon's remains were taken from Cooper Crescent to Darling Street Methodist Church. Joan remembers the occasion vividly.

The coffin was waiting in our big hall, and the Reverend Ivan Carson was standing with his back to the front door, as he said prayers and read from the Bible. The long, dying light of a beautiful summer's day was streaming in through the front door and bathing the coffin in a soft glow, as friends and family stood around. Gordon was leaving for the last time the home and the house he had so much loved. The men carried the coffin out with great dignity, and we followed on our way to the church. It was a very moving occasion, and I shall never forget it as long as I live.

On the funeral day itself the temperature in Enniskillen topped 33 degrees centigrade – among the highest temperatures in the British Isles on that day. Early that morning, Joan telephoned me at home and asked my wife Hilary and me to call in at Cooper Crescent before the funeral. We found Joan, Julie Anne and Ingrid strong and composed, as we knew they would be. Julie Anne's husband, John, was there, but he was still recovering from his motorbike accident. Other members of the family, neighbours and friends were in the house, and with typical thoughtfulness, Joan had organized a cold buffet for those who had come long distances.

As we chatted, my mind wandered to the details of the funeral service and the arrangements for the pall-bearers, and I assured myself that Gordon and Peter would, as usual, have everything under control. And then I felt a stab of shock – Gordon and Peter were dead! The mind plays strange tricks on such occasions.

The funeral in Darling Street Church had an air of *deja vu* about it. Six months earlier, the same minister, the same organist, the same friends, neighbours and public figures had gathered to say their farewell to Peter. And yet there was a world of difference. Peter's funeral had been in the depths of winter, on a grey and gloomy December day, and there had been an atmosphere of deep, heavy sadness at the tragic death of a young man who had given much to his family and church, but who still had so much to give. In the brilliant sunshine of that glorious summer's day, while there was an air of mourning at the untimely death of an exceptional and good man, there was also a thankfulness that he had been allowed to achieve so much in his life.

The church was packed, as it had been for Peter's funeral. The inside of the building was extremely hot, and the men in the congregation were invited to take off their jackets if they wished. Most of them did so, and it was a remarkable sight to see rows of white shirts around the church, on such a solemn occasion. It added a strange incongruity; it did not seem like a funeral at all.

Joan and the family took their seats in the front pew shortly before the service. As Joan walked up the aisle behind Ingrid, her two young daughters, Julie Anne and John, the same question leapt into everyone's mind: 'How much can one family bear?' But whatever Joan and the others were thinking privately, their public composure gave no hint of their inner turmoil. Dignity and restraint had always been a hallmark of the Wilsons and had held them together through so much bereavement and pain.

There was a catch in the voice of Dr Hedley Plunkett, Gordon's brother-in-law, as he read a passage from the Book of Revelation, as there had been when he read the same passage at Peter's funeral. It was just a hint of inner grief, but no more. The very simplicity of a Methodist funeral service adds to the solemnity of the occasion, with only the strong, hopeful hymns providing an outlet for churning emotions.

It was Ivan Carson's last service as Minister of Darling Street Methodist Church, since he was about to retire. He paid tribute to the Gordon we all knew so well. Even though his words of thanksgiving and hope gave comfort, it was hard not to think of the unfairness of it all. People were paying their last respects to a man who had done so much for peace and still had so much to do, and why had he not been allowed more time to carry on such important work? But even as the questions arose, the answers were partly in evidence around the church. The work of peace, so enhanced by Gordon Wilson, was not his alone. It was a task for us all.

People from very different backgrounds had joined together to pay homage to a man who had risen above political and human barriers, and in so doing they reaffirmed their recognition of the urgent need to consolidate the peace process, even if they had very different ideas as to how this might be achieved. Four visitors from Warrington, including Colin and Wendy Parry, sat in the pew normally used by the Wilson family each Sunday. Down the side of the building sat several leading Protestant and Roman Catholic clergymen, bearing witness to another important symbolism and reality. In another part of the church sat Mitchell McLaughlin, the National Chairman of Provisional Sinn Fein, whose presence symbolized something different still. It required courage on his part to attend, and also courage on the part of others to accept the symbolism of his presence, but Gordon himself would have held out the hand of friendship if he had been alive. In death, his spirit guided the entire proceedings.

There was an impressive turn-out of mourners from the Irish Republic, led by President Mary Robinson. Also present were Prime Minister John Bruton and his Deputy, Dick Spring; several ministers, including Minister of State Austin Currie; the former Prime Minister, Albert Reynolds; Bertie Ahern, the Opposition Leader; Mary Harney, the leader of the Progressive Democrats; Judge Catherine McGuinness, the Chairperson of the Forum for Peace and Reconciliation; and a number of Senators who had been Gordon's colleagues and personal friends. Their presence underlined the respect and affection which Gordon had earned from all shades of political opinion in the Republic and from the ordinary people of Ireland. It was entirely appropriate that they should be attending the funeral of an uncommon 'common' man, who had won the hearts and the respect of the nation.

The representation from Northern Ireland, though impressive enough, was not so high-powered. This was partly due to the absence of practically all of the seventeen Northern Ireland MPs and the Secretary of State, who were engaged in Northern Ireland matters at Westminster. The Government was represented by Baroness Denton and by Lady Mayhew, the wife of the Secretary of State. There were representatives from the main political parties in Northern Ireland, including the Alliance Party and the Social Democratic and Labour Party, but official representatives from the Unionist Parties were conspicuous by their absence – though two well-known Fermanagh Unionists, Harry West and Raymond Ferguson, were attending in a personal capacity.

The absence of an official Unionist representation was noticed by those who felt that Gordon deserved better in death, as he had in life, from those who had opposed him politically and had not approved of his words or actions. Their absence was particularly noted by Southern politicians. Austin Currie said: 'You would have thought that on the basis of ordinary decency, and of Christianity, the Unionists would have shown a greater appreciation and acknowledgement of Gordon's tremendous courage and Christian qualities.' Senator Mary Henry found the lack of official Unionist representatives incredible. 'They appeared to be most ungrateful. Gordon had tried valiantly to put forward the Unionist point of view in Dublin at a time when they were not prepared to speak up for themselves. They could have at least made sure that there was some kind of official representation at his funeral. I think they let themselves down by not being there.'

On the night before the funeral, Gordon's MP Ken Magennis phoned Joan to express his sympathy, and apologized for being unable to attend the funeral due to urgent Westminster business. Joan accepted his expression of sympathy and his apology, and chose to let the matter rest. She said later: 'What mattered to me most was that Gordon's friends, who wanted to be there, were at the funeral.' People have their own reasons for choosing to go or to stay away from a funeral, but the Unionists should have shown more respect for and generosity towards a man who had tried honourably and courageously to promote peace and reconciliation, even if they did not approve of the way he went about it.

Such considerations, however, were of secondary importance as the funeral cortege wound its way from the church and paused briefly at the Enniskillen Cenotaph, where Gordon and Marie had lain under the rubble on that awful Remembrance Sunday. So much had happened since then. There had been so much suffering, and yet so much good had developed from the horror. As Gordon's coffin was laid to rest beside Marie's in the scorching summer heat, the deep sadness of those gathered around the grave was tempered by another reality, that after all his turmoil and heartache, Gordon was at peace.

I thought of his anguish on the night when Marie died, and the words that were carried around the world: *'Don't ask me, please, for a purpose. I don't have a purpose. I don't have an answer. But I know there has to be a plan. It's part of a greater plan, and God is good. And we shall meet again.'* As I slowly walked away from Gordon's grave, I knew that Joan and Julie Anne and Ingrid were sustained by their Christian belief that somehow and somewhere beyond the barriers of rationality and of time, beyond death itself, the circle had been completed. The grave had no victory. Gordon and Marie and Peter had met again.

Back at the Methodist church hall, people had gathered for tea. Over in one corner of the room Joan and Julie Anne were speaking to friends and others who had come to pay their last respects to Gordon. Earlier they had met President Mary Robinson and Government leaders. In another part of the church hall, Mitchell McLaughlin was in deep conversation with two Protestants who were well known for their reconciliation work in the community. The vital work of bridge-building was going on. One by one the mourners said their farewells and set off for home on that beautiful summer's evening. It had been a sombre day, yet the scorching heat and the dazzling light had lent it a surreal quality. It seemed impossible to believe that Gordon Wilson was dead and buried.

As the evening wore on, Joan gathered her family around her, and they went back to Cooper Crescent, with its happy memories of children growing up and the ordinary normality of everyday lives, which later seem so extraordinary when some of the pillars of that family have disappeared. Joan would never be totally alone, yet so much had been taken from her. But she had shown great resilience in the past, and she would do so again.

As she said herself: 'It was like being on a long walk with three people who were literally a part of you, and each time you looked back one of them had gone. Even though I had been through the trauma of Marie's death, and then Peter's death, I still could not believe that they had really gone, and that Gordon had gone as well. It was like a dream. I felt myself becoming frightened, not knowing what to do, but I also knew that the others needed me, and that we were still a family. I had no option but to put my best foot forward and to carry on, in the strength of the Lord.'

16

An Ordinary Hero

Despite Joan's strength and firm resolution, she was devastated by Gordon's death, and although she never once lost her composure in public, she grieved and wept in private. She was ever conscious of her key role at the centre of the family, as the parent, mother-in-law and grandmother who could use her experience in helping the others to come to terms with multiple loss in a tragically short period of time. But she could not be with them all the time, nor they with her, and of necessity she was alone for long periods. She had retired from her job as a music teacher some months earlier in order to be able to spend more time with Gordon; now his death had robbed her of that too.

The house at Cooper Crescent is large, and for one person it can seem vast, lonely and intimidating. At one point Joan had an over-whelming urge to sell up and leave, in order to make a new start else-where. The family persuaded her to stay, partly as Cooper Crescent is just across the road from Enniskillen Collegiate and therefore well placed for Joan's granddaughters to drop in to see her after school each day. The family also feared that if Joan moved to a new district she would find it hard to settle in, and that she would badly miss her neigh-bours, who had been such a tower of strength through her successive bereavements. Deep down Joan knew that they were right, and although she could be as determined and strong-minded as Gordon had been, she took their advice and stayed. Her only compromise was to have her kitchen newly fitted out. It has beautiful views and it is the hub of the household.

In the early days after Gordon's death, Joan busied herself around the house and kept herself occupied with all sorts of tasks to try to forget her loneliness. At night she kept all the lights on until bedtime, to ward off the encroaching darkness, and for weeks she moved from bedroom to bedroom to try to find some solace in sleep. During the day she listened to her beloved classical music, which she found brought her a sense of peace and spiritual renewal. At first she could only listen to Mozart, but gradually, as the aching eased, she turned to Bach and to Beethoven as well. An accomplished pianist, she often played on the baby-grand piano in the living-room, and this too brought comfort and relaxation. She continued in her role as choir-mistress at Darling Street Methodist Church. She says: 'This helped to give me direction and purpose. The choir will never know how important each member has been to me.'

A few days after the funeral, the family took a short holiday at picturesque Portballinatrae, where the Atlantic breakers meet the North Antrim coast. It had been a favourite summer resort when the children were small, and the memories came flooding back. Joan says: 'We talked, we cried together, and as before we found great healing beside the ocean.' Back home in Enniskillen, Joan continued her regular walks around the spacious grounds of Castle Coole, a beautiful National Trust property, and here she often met local townspeople who exchanged a few words of greeting and sympathy or, more often, she was able to enjoy on her own the quiet beauties of nature. She says: 'Many a tear I have shed at Castle Coole, and my advice to anyone grieving in this way is simply to let go. Your tears also have healing powers.'

Tears sometimes came without warning. There were good days, especially when bright weather helped to lift her spirits. There were also bad, dreary days when she would find herself back in the pit of despair. 'Sometimes I would panic at having to do the most ordinary things, such as going into local shops. But I had to pull myself together and get on with it. There was no alternative. I remember the first time that I went out on my own and did a morning's shopping I felt a real sense of achievement. I said to myself on the way home, "Gordon would be proud of you!"'

Only once did she dream about Gordon. 'He was looking well, and in my dream he was helping to organize me – as usual! I was going out to open a church sale, and he seemed to be pointing at his watch and saying, "You're doing well, but be careful about your time." He gave me his big, broad smile, as if to let me know he was all right, and then he had gone. It was dreadful to have to wake up and to discover that it had been a dream, but having seen him like that and looking so well, I felt strangely comforted.'

The first Easter Sunday after Gordon's death was particularly difficult. Easter Day, with its great celebration of resurrection, had always been a special day in the Wilson home. Without Gordon, Joan felt restless and alone. 'After a beautiful service in church, I went to his grave and to Marie's and then to Peter's, but I could not find peace. Julie Anne and her family were out for the afternoon, and eventually I went to my next-door neighbour, Edna Young, and asked her to go with me for a walk, and that helped.' Joan was yet again learning the hard truth of her experience that 'time does not heal, it only teaches you how to cope a bit better'.

The passing months also provided an opportunity for Gordon's family, friends and colleagues to look back on his life and achievements, with a clearer perspective. The obituaries and leading articles in the newspapers immediately after his death reflected some of the views of the general public about a man who had so caught the headlines. The London *Times* described him as 'one of Ireland's most substantial peace campaigners', though it noted that in his decision to meet the IRA 'there seemed to be a quality of exaggerated idealism about him which bordered on naivety.' *The Belfast Telegraph* stated that 'Gordon Wilson would be the last to admit it, but he helped to turn the tide towards peace in our times.' The London *Independent* made the point that 'Over the past year, Gordon Wilson may have had the comfort of reflecting that the tragedy of Enniskillen planted a seed which, years afterwards, helped his country to move from war to peace.'

All of these comments were true, but such reflections of the public perception of Gordon Wilson as a peacemaker fail to take into account also the inner complexity of the man. He was a headline-maker, and he had a gift for plain, direct communication, but he was no simple do-gooder. He was hailed as a hero, yet he always described himself as an ordinary man. He was determined, hard-headed, impatient, demanding, charming, perceptive, visionary, humorous, courageous and genuinely forgiving – an extraordinarily 'ordinary' man indeed.

He tried hard to present himself as being 'ordinary' because he truly believed that he *was* ordinary. This was well summarized in his submission to the Sinn Fein Peace Forum in February 1994. He stated:

> I am a very ordinary sort of man. I have few personal ambitions and no political aspirations. I just want to live and let live. Life has been kind to me in the main, and I have tried to live by the [Good] Book. I do not profess to be a good man, but I aim to be. I would like to leave the world a better place than I found it, but I have no exaggerated ideas of my ability to do so. I have hitched my wagon to a star – a star of hope, the star of Bethlehem.

Gordon's perception of himself was accurate enough, but, like most of us, he had blind spots about his own complexity – which his family and friends could see. He was sentimental to the point of sometimes being reduced to tears by a film on television, but he was also a hard-headed businessman who made a good living by selling clothes to Protestants and Roman Catholics in an Ulster border town. He could be utterly charming and gracious, but he could push his family (and friends) to the limit by his hard-edged impatience and sometimes unreasonable demands. He related extremely well to women, and they to him (he had an avuncular eye for a pretty girl!), but he could also be an old-fashioned male chauvinist. He showed a profound depth of practical Christianity, but he was also a most taxing companion after a bad day's golf. He was a strict Methodist, but unlike most committed Wesleyans, he smoked heavily and he was fond of an occasional tipple in the right company. He did not court the media, but neither did he mind being in the spotlight. He was a little shy but he could also be a show-off. In short, he had more than a spark of the divine, but he was also very human.

As a politician he was often underestimated by his critics, and by some commentators, as an amateur among professionals. In reality, the professionals recognized that while he would never be an orthodox party man, his political skills were enviable. Aisling Maguire, his assistant in Dublin, noted: 'He was no mere do-gooder, he made us all sit up and think.' His major speeches to the Senate and the Forum were well shaped, powerfully and emotionally delivered, and listened to attentively by politicians who had had a lifetime's experience in public speaking.

His political stances were always carefully thought out. For example, his views on the future unity of Ireland, which were so clearly set out in his position paper to the Forum for Peace and Reconciliation, were not the result of a whim or of a desire to grab the headlines, as they inevitably did. In a lengthy and important speech to the Senate on 7 July 1994 he concentrated on the same theme and stated: 'It seems to me that there are two essential identities in Ireland, and beyond that a strange and not quite yet born other identity. In an odd way we are all Irish, although some of my Northern countrymen deny Irishness. I regret this denial but it is a fact of life.'

It was this dual nationality – his claim that he was both British and Irish – which puzzled many people on both sides of the border. Most Northern Protestants, the vast majority of whom are Unionists, take a typically straightforward view: you are either British or Irish, you cannot be both. Southerners, who can be more subtle on some aspects of their politics, would agree on this point – though it is interesting to note that some institutions in the South retain the 'Royal' prefix – such as the Royal Dublin Society. Gordon, however, saw no distinction. His feeling that he was both British and Irish may have stemmed from his early years and from the influence of his parents, who themselves were brought up in an Ireland that had been united under British rule. He believed that the partition of Ireland in the early twenties not only created two states, but also two identities. He said in a keynote Senate speech:

We must also accept that partition has, in a strange and unexpected way, worked to a degree. It has divided North from South, if that is what it was intended to do. Southern Protestants are not as Northern Protestants; they accept the democracy of the Irish

Republic. Similarly, Northern Catholics are not as Southern
Catholics and have not the latter's sense of autonomy and, to an
extent, the all-too-common Southerner's incomprehension of his
Northern brethren, regardless of religion.

Despite the differences, he did not see these two parts of the island 'as
being foreign to each other. I believe passionately that we are all the
same people, but we quarrel and we have quarrelled tragically. I know: I
lost a daughter.' He told Senate members that he was proud to be
British and Irish, and he assured them that his dual identity was honestly held and honestly defended. 'I say this as someone who loves Ireland
and who knows the Republic almost as well as he knows the North and
who loves both.' While such statements perplexed and even angered his
Unionist friends and acquaintances in the North, they made his Southern friends think much more deeply about the complexities of attitudes
North of the border. To this extent he made a valuable contribution to a
search for better cross-border understanding, and his whole life was a
witness to a new kind of peaceful Ireland that might some day emerge.

He was perhaps one of the first prototype Irishmen of the twenty-first
century, equally at home with a dual passport and dual nationality, and
seeing each tradition not as a threat to one or the other but as a base on
which to build the best for both, and for the benefit of all. Significantly,
he was not dewy-eyed about this, or about the practical difficulties
involved. Certainly, he had no illusions about the massive uphill struggle required to encourage people to think differently, on all sides. At the
end of his Senate speech on 7 July 1994 he said: 'To fire relevant hard-
hitting questions at one's own community and tradition requires far
more courage than to fire bullets or to plant bombs. Let those who carry
arms lay them down.'

In a perceptive and toughly-worded article in the *Sunday Times* on
4 September 1994, a few days after the IRA ceasefire was announced,
he noted that during the previous general election the people of his con-
stituency in Northern Ireland had had a choice to vote for 'Sinn Fein
and the gun' or to vote for the SDLP. He stated: 'Half of them chose the
gun. I know that every second Catholic I meet has voted for the gun.

I never know which ones, yet the Catholic community has been totally supportive of my stance.' These are not the words of a romantic dreamer, but the insights of a hard-headed political realist. Gordon Wilson knew only too well the difficulties of trying to change attitudes in his native land.

While Gordon was politically shrewd, he never claimed to know all the answers. At times his confidence and assurance dissolved into near despair, as when he called for the internment without trial of paramilitary leaders, following what he thought was his abortive meeting with the IRA. In October 1993 he told the Senate, after a period of savage blood-letting in the North, 'We're in a civil war situation now, not approaching it.' His family and friends were worried at times that he would venture out of his depth in political matters. It would have been all too easy for this man who had made the moral high ground his own to lose his way in the frequently dirty business of politics.

Deep inside himself he worried about this too. He was supremely confident and sure of himself when telling Marie's story, but politics was a different matter. On more than one occasion he asked me, and no doubt other close friends, 'How can I go on saying the same things about the lessons of Enniskillen, again and again and again?' My answer was always the same and always direct: 'You have no choice. The events of Enniskillen and your reaction to those events have placed you on high moral ground. You must keep on saying those things again and again, because they contain eternal truths about love and forgiveness, and because they cannot be repeated often enough. Whether you like it or not, you have become an icon, a symbol of hope and forgiveness. And you have to weigh up all of that against becoming involved in the rough and tumble of daily politics.'

It was an answer he never liked, but he was practical enough to heed this and other advice. He did not like being described as an icon. He would say: 'That's a load of old nonsense', but he accepted that there was some truth in it. For example, in his keynote speech at the opening of the Forum for Peace and Reconciliation, he emphasized that he was marching 'to the beat of another drum – not the drums of war but of peace'. He felt that he was representing '"the ordinary people" of this land, both North and South, who are weary of conflict and are crying out for peace'.

He literally wore himself out working for peace. No journey was too far, no meeting was too long, if he thought it would help to further the peace process. He used to confide in his political and other friends, 'I can get an audience with almost anyone. How can I use this to further peace?' He made a number of private visits to London, and he told no one about them, not even Joan. He had ready access to high places, including palaces and presidential residences, and the private offices of prime ministers, but he was a discreet person and very rarely mentioned such visits, which lesser men would have been glad to boast about.

In November 1993 he had a secret two-hour meeting with representatives of Loyalist paramilitary groups, on the Shankill Road in Belfast. This followed the initiative of Methodist clergymen who felt that such a meeting might bear fruit, after a period of intense paramilitary killing on both sides. During his meeting with the Loyalist paramilitaries, Gordon was accompanied by two Methodist clergymen and a former paramilitary who had become a Christian and had renounced violence. On the other side there were three representatives, including one man who later became a well-known and articulate exponent of the Loyalist paramilitary viewpoint.

The meeting went well, contrary to garbled press speculation afterwards. One of those present recalls that Gordon immediately put the Loyalists at ease by saying, 'Don't be using any big words, because big words still stump me!' The Loyalists were moved by what Gordon had to say, and according to one witness, they were deeply impressed by his sincerity and integrity. He, for his part, was impressed by their articulate presentation and by their clear and, in his opinion, balanced analysis of the situation.

He was convinced that they were not anti-Catholic, that they had accepted that everyone would have to learn to coexist peaceably on the island of Ireland, and that they were committed to parity of esteem on all sides. Gordon believed that if the IRA could be persuaded to lay down their arms, the Loyalists would follow suit, because their leaders felt that violence was no longer a part of the equation. One of the clergymen conveyed this message to the IRA through an intermediary, but the answer came back that the Provisionals were not ready to lay down arms at that point, and the opportunity was lost. Those present at the Shankill Road meeting agreed that it had been worthwhile, and decided to come together again, but they were overtaken by events, and no further encounter took place. Gordon, however, had shown his willingness to act as an honest broker, and this was typical of the efforts he was making behind the scenes, as well as in public, to further the peace process.

In any analysis of Gordon Wilson's life and achievements, four main qualities stand out: his abundant charm, his practical shrewdness, his great courage and his outstanding Christianity. He had the folksy charm of a countryman who was an accomplished storyteller, with a good sense of humour, and who was equally at ease in the company of both men and women. He could be a man's man, and yet his sensitivity and charm appealed to women of all ages. Gordon liked people, and they liked him. Strangers who came to see him, expecting to meet a rather sad, saintly or 'other-worldly' man, were bowled over by his directness, warmth and humour.

His shrewdness spoke for itself. He had built up a thriving business in a mixed community where he combined a cheery word to everyone with a steely resolve not to take sides and to go right down the middle. He was not only wise, but street-wise as well. And when he was thrust into the tough world of politics and the media, he hardly put a foot wrong, despite all the pressures. Though he was a man of great sensitivity and of transparent emotion, as when his face told all the story, his earthy practicality and his uncommon common sense saw him through almost every situation.

His courage was unquestionable, though few people realized the depth of courage he required to live through the traumas which weighed so heavily on him, after Marie's death. He showed courage in so many different ways and to so many differing degrees – when he lay under the rubble of the Enniskillen bomb, holding Marie's hand, in the hospital afterwards and later that evening in taking on media interviews; he showed courage in fighting his way back to a semblance of normal life, in taking his seat in the Senate, in meeting the IRA face to face, and in squaring up to the unspeakable tragedy of Peter's death. He was courageous, too, in bearing silently the many criticisms of those who thought that he was naive and misguided. He would only say to Joan privately, and wearily, 'Those people cannot even begin to comprehend what I've been through.' He was particularly hurt by the criticisms of the relatives of the others killed and injured in the Enniskillen bomb, and by the indifference or the studied silence of his friends who disapproved of him taking his seat in the Irish Senate.

Denzil McDaniel, the editor of the *Impartial Reporter* in Enniskillen, worked closely with Gordon during his years in politics, and he was acutely aware of the strains he felt. 'In his home county, he probably evoked more criticism than from outside. Although not wishing to be too harsh in their criticism of him publicly, often families of other victims of violence would be quite hard in having a go at his comments in private. What they often didn't realize was that Gordon himself was acutely aware that he could offend them, and he often made the point that he spoke only for himself.' Gordon many times requested that the *Impartial Reporter* would carry his speech or statement in full, in case something could be taken out of context. Yet Denzil McDaniel says: 'Never once did he ask for criticism to be curtailed or held back in any way.' Gordon Wilson was indeed a man of immense physical and moral courage, but these very qualities, as well as his remarkable gift for communication, often got him into trouble.

David Bolton, a social worker from Enniskillen who helped the victims of the bombing, underlines Gordon's ability to communicate: 'He always seemed to have the right word for the moment. So when a microphone was pushed under his nose, he did not allow himself to be flattered but said what he thought, and he was worth listening to. He frequently made comments which cut through the political posturing and with which many could identify.'

This, however, posed problems. He was often asked for his views when others who had been affected by the bombing were not. They too had a story to tell, and usually they had no opportunity to tell it. Gordon and members of his family were often invited to public occasions.

He did not know that other bereaved families had not been invited, but this apparent exclusion was hurtful to them. He was seen by some to be assuming a place over and above his station, and on occasion he was accused of 'acting the big fella'. In response he drew attention to his limitations, but that did not stop him from using the many opportunities he was given to speak his mind, usually with great effect.

When he expressed his views, he said what he thought, and that was not always what Unionist people wanted to hear. This made him unpopular in Unionist circles. His generosity was a constant embarrassment to militant Republicans as well. There were times when it seemed he could please no one, and his public role was often a lonely one.

As a result of his ability to say something meaningful, he was often asked to comment on religious issues, which disconcerted him. People wanted him to say things that stirred them and moved them. They looked to him for inspiration, but he never for a moment regarded himself as a moral or religious leader.

He had a clearer idea of his abilities and limitations after he had produced *Marie: a Story from Enniskillen*. By the time he joined the Senate he was very much his own man with his own views. He was able to stand against those who either intentionally or otherwise abused his good will and he could hold his own forthrightly and directly.

Gordon was, by any standards, a remarkable Christian. He had been a good, salt-of-the-earth, 'ordinary' Christian in Enniskillen for many years before the bomb. After the explosion his Christianity was put to the test in full view of the world's media. His comments after Marie's death were born out of the white heat of suffering. There was no time for a finely judged response; his words came straight from his heart. And he never wavered on that central point of forgiveness and love. He will be remembered, above all, for the words he spoke that night.

Yet it did not end there. In interview after interview, talk after talk he hammered home the need for forgiveness and love. The 'Marie story' became his life's mission; it dominated him completely. Each time he told it, the story had a new urgency and a new freshness, and he was always searching for new ways to express it. In one of his last public appearances, in York, just a few weeks before he died, he ended by asking himself and his audience, 'Who is my neighbour? And the answer I get is that my neighbour is not just the lady next door, or my Protestant neighbour or my Catholic neighbour. Mankind is my neighbour, you are my neighbour, and my neighbour must also include my terrorist neighbour, because Christ died for him or her too.'

This was not a sudden inspiration or invention, but part of the very fabric of the man; it lay at the centre of his beliefs. A year earlier he had made the same point, at a meeting held in the Christian Renewal Centre in Rostrevor. That evening is recalled nostalgically by the Reverend Cecil Kerr, the Director of the Centre and a friend of Gordon's:

> I treasure the memory of the last words I heard him speak in Rostrevor as the sun went down over the tranquil waters of Carlingford Lough, an invisible line in the inlet marking the border of our divided island. He read the immortal words of the world's greatest forgiver, Jesus: 'Love the Lord your God with all your heart, with all your soul and with all your mind. This is the first and greatest commandment. And the second is like it: Love your neighbour as yourself.' And Gordon gently added, 'My neighbour is mankind, my neighbour must include my terrorist neighbour, for Christ died for them too.'

Gordon's article in the *Sunday Times* returned to this theme. He referred to Marie's last words about love which, he wrote, 'burned a hole in my heart'. That made him think of loving his neighbour, even terrorists. And then came the typically humorous, practical and earthy Wilson twist: 'It is not easy: you do not have to like them but you have to try and love them.'

Julie Anne, who is so like her father, sums up his achievements simply and eloquently: 'He made a real difference to the situation and to this country. He made a lot of people think, and he made them realize that peace could be so much better than the endless killing of innocent people. He did not just talk about it, he actually did something about it. He really did cherish peace, and he knew in his heart that peace would come.' And in a rare moment of self-revelation she said, 'I am extraordinarily proud of him, more so than anyone can ever know. I could not describe to anyone just how enormously proud of him I am.'

Gordon was without doubt an extraordinarily 'ordinary' hero, but Joan has heroic qualities of her own. She would be the first to deny it, but many people – not just her family and close friends – see her that way. It was Joan who deliberately chose to stay in the background after Marie's death and to support Gordon in his public mission. She shared his grief, and she supported him in all the important decisions – not least in his decisions to take his seat in the Irish Senate and, later, to confront the IRA directly. She stayed at home and held the family together when he was taken up in a whirl of public engagements, and when he came back home, full of the varied experiences he had shared with important people, she gently steered him back to earth. Without Joan, Gordon could not have achieved what he did. Even today she is reluctant to take credit for the part she played, or to minimize in any way Gordon's achievements. She says simply, and with a smile, 'We were a very good team.'

Her rock-like faith remains unshaken: 'I have never blamed God, because I believe that he has a hand in everything. There is a purpose in all that happens. There is a time to be born and a time to die, and there is a completeness about things. Gordon was taken at his prime, at his peak, but God felt that his mission had been accomplished. He had health and wholeness of mind. I dread to think what would have happened if he had been left paralysed or badly incapacitated in any way. Gordon would not have been a good patient. He would have found that terribly hard to bear.'

She becomes angry when people describe her as 'a poor widow'. She says: 'I have not yet thought of myself as a "widow" and I don't think I ever will. And I am certainly not "poor". I have a wealth of riches all around me – my family, my friends, my neighbours, my music. I am anything but "a poor widow".' She is hurt by people who ask, 'How are you?' and then don't stop to listen. 'It's often the people who have suffered themselves who are prepared to take time to listen to you, because they know what suffering is like. The others don't even realize that you have already noticed that they don't really want to hear you.'

She still prays for the bombers who killed Marie, that they might repent and seek God's pardon and forgiveness. She says: 'I would still like to meet them and to ask them face to face, "Why did you do a thing like that?" I would say to them, "There is a better way, which is God's way, and you will have no peace unless you seek his forgiveness. Whether you believe in God or not, some day you will have to face his judgement."' Joan says she could not come to Holy Communion if she felt enmity for anyone. 'We are told to forgive those who trespass against us. Those are our orders, and God will give us strength to carry them out.'

Joan finds great comfort in writing letters to those who have lost loved ones, and also in receiving letters, including those from complete strangers – most often women – who write to her. On the first Easter after Gordon died she received a letter from a Mrs Joyce Thomas in Wales, who said she was thinking about her, and included a five-pound note, 'to buy yourself something, just as a little treat'. Joan says, 'I was immensely touched by that.'

Another typical letter came from Katharine Cheney of Banbury, just after Remembrance Sunday. She wrote:

> I've been thinking of you, especially over the past year, when both Peter and Gordon have died – and I thought I would write and tell you so. I hope you are keeping well in yourself, and have some good friends around. Anniversaries come and go – and once again we have been reminded of Enniskillen on Remembrance Day – but you are remembered in the in-between times as well.

Joan says, 'This gives me so much comfort, to think that people are thinking about me and taking the trouble to write.'

She also appreciates the fact that Gordon's friends in Dublin still keep in touch with her. Senator Mary Henry phones her regularly, and Judge Catherine McGuinness invited her to the Forum for Peace and Reconciliation on the morning it was addressed by the South African Deputy President, F. W. de Klerk. That afternoon, President Mary Robinson invited her to afternoon tea at her official residence in

Dublin. She thinks highly of Joan, as she did of Gordon. 'I am very fond of Joan, not only for herself but for what she was for Gordon. She was his rock. He needed her deeply and she was always there for him. At Gordon's funeral I said to Joan, "It's better that he went first and not you. He wouldn't have been able to cope without you."'

Joan, for her part, is overwhelmed by the kindness and thoughtfulness of her many friends and of Gordon's old friends, but nevertheless, the bad times still come and go. The slightest thing can trigger off a memory or bring the tears. 'I don't know how people cope with bereavement without a Christian faith. I would have committed suicide by now if I had not truly believed that God was with me through it all. For a long time I refused to let go of Marie. I wanted her back so much, but now I have learned to leave her in God's care, and Peter and Gordon too. That helps to ease the pain and bring me a sense of peace, but the aching loneliness is always there, like a frost of sorrows. But I know that so many others have suffered and are suffering, and my heart goes out to them. I am sad, and sometimes lonely, but I am not afraid, for I know that God is with me and that he will supply all my needs.' Joan is in no hurry to map out the future. 'If God has a purpose for me, he will guide me accordingly.' In the meantime, her life is full enough with her family and her music, and with her concern, love and prayers for others.

She misses Gordon. She misses his voice, his presence around the house, his stories about the characters in the Senate and the Dail, his laughter and his guiding strength. 'We were both strong-minded people and sometimes the sparks flew, behind closed doors! But we were good to and for each other. Now I realize even more the important things of life. Gordon taught me so much. He gave me self-confidence, and above all he showed me that the bottom line really is love. I am only touching the tip of the iceberg, but I am learning. The rough edges are being knocked off, that's for sure. Some of the things which used to seem so important are simply not important any more. People ask me what have I learned, at the end of it all, and my reply is simple but from the heart. It is this: "I know that my Redeemer liveth."'

At the end of his book *Marie*, Gordon used these words:

The first and last words in this whole story are about love. That's what helps me to keep going, to get through my days and to sleep at night. Love God and your neighbour. In life and after death there's only one ultimate standard by which we are judged. Marie showed that, to us all, as she lay under the rubble at the Cenotaph holding my hand, with her life slipping away. The bottom line is love. There's nothing more I can say.

Gordon and Joan Wilson and their family, in life and in death, have indeed said it all.